Praise for *Old Dog, New [Dog]*

"A perfect collaboration.... Each author is acutely aware of the unique needs of dogs who are in the life stage of their specialty, so the text is able to advocate equally strongly for the new pup, the senior dog, *and* the humans who will need to juggle and balance the dogs' needs!"
— *Whole Dog Journal*

"This book achieves what is to me a literary miracle: It is a fascinating read that moves quickly yet is dense with practical, useful advice. I have been a professional dog trainer for over forty years, and I absorbed advice in these pages that I didn't anticipate needing or gaining. I knew immediately upon starting it that it would become my go-to recommendation for anyone with a senior dog, a middle-aged dog (to give them time to prep), or a puppy — whether or not the old dog and the new dog will overlap."
— **Sue Sternberg**, canine behavior specialist, shelter owner, and author

"Kathy and Helen have joined forces to create this incredible, much-needed resource for the dog lovers out there who share their lives with a beloved aging dog and are considering adopting another. As a perfect team, they answer with articulate simplicity the questions you may have about whether or not to take this step, and how to set yourself and your canine companions up for success."
— **Pat Miller**, CBCC-KA, CPDT-KA, bestselling author of *The Power of Positive Dog Training*

"This collaboration is a gift to both dog professionals and caregivers alike. *Old Dog, New Dog* is the book I wish I'd had eight years ago, when, heartbroken from the loss of one senior dog, we transitioned a puppy in with our remaining senior. The authors have created an essential playbook for managing this phase with care and grace. As a human well-being specialist, I appreciate their

attention to the complex emotions involved — and their thoughtful approach to balancing joy and sorrow."
— **Marlene O'Neill Laberge**, MSW, LFDM, organizational health and well-being specialist, Ruff Relationships

"How wonderful that such compassionate, knowledgeable experts have joined forces to lead us through the seasons of multi-dog households! *Old Dog, New Dog* is a unique resource, full of practical tips that help dog families navigate life together, from potty time to pain relief."
— **Wendy Lyons Sunshine**, FDM, author of *Tender Paws: How Science-Based Parenting Can Transform Our Relationships with Dogs*

"This is an essential read for anyone pondering the decision of adding another dog to a household with a senior dog. The authors provide a comprehensive look at the emotional and practical considerations from all perspectives — the new dog's, the senior dog's, and the humans'."
— **Jennifer Shryock**, CDBC, LFDM, founder of Family Paws

"Trainers and veterinarians will be very thankful to have this thought-provoking, easy-to-digest resource to place in the hands and hearts of their clients who are thinking about getting a puppy to raise alongside their aging dog."
— **Marc Bekoff**, PhD, author of *Dogs Demystified* and *The Emotional Lives of Animals*

"The authors' years of experience working with dogs at either end of the age spectrum shine in this practical and succinct guide. This is a must-read for every pet guardian who is considering adding a new puppy to their home while facing the sadness of saying goodbye to a beloved older four-legged family member."
— **Viviane Arzoumanian**, LFDM, CDBC, CPDT-KA, founder of PumpkinPups Dog Training

OLD DOG, NEW DOG

OLD DOG, NEW DOG

Supporting Your Aging Best Friend and Welcoming a New One

Kathy Callahan and Helen St. Pierre

Foreword by Kim Brophey

New World Library
Novato, California

New World Library
14 Pamaron Way
Novato, California 94949

Copyright © 2025 by Kathy Callahan and Helen St. Pierre

All rights reserved. This book may not be reproduced in whole or in part, stored in a retrieval system, or transmitted in any form or by any means — electronic, mechanical, or other — without written permission from the publisher, except by a reviewer, who may quote brief passages in a review.

The material in this book is intended for education. It is not meant to take the place of diagnosis and treatment by a qualified veterinary practitioner or trainer. No expressed or implied guarantee of the effects of the use of the recommendations can be given nor liability taken.

Text design by Tona Pearce Myers

Library of Congress Cataloging-in-Publication data is available.

First printing, June 2025
ISBN 978-1-60868-996-5
Ebook ISBN 978-1-60868-997-2
Printed in Canada

10   9   8   7   6   5   4   3   2   1

New World Library is committed to protecting our natural environment. This book is made of material from well-managed FSC®-certified forests and other controlled sources.

Contents

Foreword by Kim Brophey..................................ix

Preface...xiii

Chapter One
Supporting Your Senior..................................1

Chapter Two
Welcoming a Puppy.....................................33

Chapter Three
Managing a Senior and a Puppy, Together........57

Chapter Four
Adding an Adult Dog Instead of a Puppy..........81

Chapter Five
Savoring the Sunset....................................91

Chapter Six
Starting the Next Chapter...........................113

Acknowledgments..119

Index..122

About the Authors......................................128

Foreword

One of the hardest things to accept is that the truth in any given situation is usually full of paradoxes. We're always seeking clarity in our perceptions — clarity that could guide us to the "right" decisions. In this quest for black-and-white answers, we discover again and again just how darn gray, complicated, messy, and even seemingly contradictory life's chapters can actually be. Thank goodness we have the likes of Helen St. Pierre and Kathy Callahan to take our hand and walk us through at least one of them.

Reading this book in the same year that I have both said goodbye to a beloved senior dog and introduced a new puppy, I am profoundly grateful that the world's dog lovers will have such a valuable guide for their own beautifully bittersweet moments in the circle of life. Dogs inevitably force us to face hard lessons of love, as canine lives are far too short for the uniquely powerful bonds we build with them and for our dreams of growing old *together*. We're doomed to be repeatedly robbed of the happily-ever-after fantasy we stubbornly embrace with every canine friendship we welcome into our family. But our optimism prevails, each new wagging tail igniting a retelling of the love story we humans share with our dogs. For most of us, to know the power of a love shared with a dog is to be unable to live without it.

As the chapters of our canine companions' lives unfold, we find ourselves with fewer pages ahead than behind. We know that we're nearing the end of the story, but we want it to go on. We don't just want a new book; we want a sequel. How do we weave the stories together in an epic series, so that each dog may live on through the next?

Kathy and Helen provide a beacon of light for us to follow, with pragmatic and thoughtful consideration for the senior dogs and new youngsters alike (as well as our own human experiences in these often-challenging moments). With sensitivity to the distinctly different needs of aging canines and developing puppies, they offer invaluable insights and detailed, practical approaches that will lead to best-case outcomes for those who find themselves at this common crossroads. More importantly, they urge us to recognize the importance of ensuring that every family member has the quality of life that they deserve — a good life. Combining and distilling a vast body of animal behavior and welfare science with industry best practices, the authors rightly assert that our dogs need and deserve a standard-of-life functioning, meaningful sense of purpose, and experiences of true joy — giving us the nuts and bolts we need to make the best decisions at the critical junctures.

This book fills an empty space on the bookshelf of every dog lover out there, providing a pattern for us to follow as we enter the agonizing and thrilling paradox of letting go

Foreword

of and welcoming these treasured friends. Our love stories with our dogs will be all the richer for the lessons we learn from these two invaluable leaders in the dog world, as we each add stories to our libraries of love called dogs.

— Kim Brophey, CDBC, CPDT-KA, LFDM,
applied ethologist, behavior consultant and trainer,
author of *Meet Your Dog*, and developer of the
L.E.G.S. model of canine science

Preface

One of us specializes in puppies, the other in old dogs. Because of that, there are two questions we both get over and over — and if you're holding this book in your hands, it's likely that one of the two is on your mind:

1. "Our dog is getting older. Should we get a puppy now, or is it too late?"
2. "We thought our old dog would love a new puppy, but we were wrong! What do we do now?"

While the two of us come at the "old dog, new dog" issue from opposite ends of the age spectrum, we've always offered the same answer to both questions: "It depends."

We know: That isn't very helpful!

So we decided to fill in the blanks and write a book together. What, exactly, does it depend on? And how can people increase their odds of making good decisions, following up with excellent management and care, creating a beautiful sunset for their senior, and embarking on a continuation of their wonderful dog tradition with a new addition to the family?

There are plenty of books that dive deep on either puppies or aging dogs, but it's different to consider each alongside the other. In the following pages, we will help you do just that.

— Kathy Callahan and Helen St. Pierre

Chapter One

Supporting Your Senior

A quietly shocking truth sneaks up on the luckiest dog people, and it's this: Nothing compares to the companionship of a senior dog. If you already know this, then another truth may have dawned on you: Your friend is aging.

Our graying, snoring, shuffling friends have been with us through it all. Their faces are woven through our photos, their presence a constant in our memories. They've greeted us with joy every time we've walked through the door. They've helped build our circles, weighing in on friends, relatives, and potential spouses. They've turned the couch into our happy place and given hiking a purpose. They've welcomed first babies, and later walked them to the bus. Their fur has absorbed the tears from the bad days, the breakups, and the scary test results.

By the time their muzzles have grayed, they're not just our dogs anymore. They have become our teachers, our therapists, and — for sure — our family. They carry a connection to our history that grounds us, and a wisdom that brings peace and calm to our home.

At this point, you will find that you want to slow down time, but you can't. What you can do, though, is rise to the occasion. Rather than pretend it's not happening or wish it away, you can equip yourself to truly be there for your dog just like your dog has always been there for you. You can learn to smooth out the hard parts about getting older and make this stage beautifully rewarding for you both. Just as humans need to lean on family more as they age, so do dogs. Their world will get a little bit smaller, but that doesn't mean they have to experience less joy and love. That part is up to you.

"Wait — Is My Dog Already a Senior?"

Time flies. That's why it can be a shock the first time a veterinarian casually suggests it's time for "senior food." What? Surely your sweet pup can't already be considered old? You remember your first day with her like it was yesterday!

But indeed, dog years fly, and this casual conversation with the vet begs the question "When is a dog considered old?" Long ago, there was always a chart hanging in the vet clinic that said if our dog was a certain size, and over a certain age, boom: She's a senior. But these days we know it's not that simple. As our understanding of dogs and their health has deepened, we've become better able to assess aging for each individual. After all, plenty of fourteen-year-old dogs act just as full of life as they did at six, while others are clearly beginning to slow down at seven. Age itself is not a disease.

For dog owners, the most helpful definition of a senior is this one: A senior is a dog past the physical prime of her life. It's when aging has begun to slow her ability to act as she once did. The new physical limitations may come from disease, metabolic changes, or both. Either way, once they start to encroach on a dog's normal movements, activities, or routine, it makes sense to view a dog as entering her "senior" phase of life.

Nobody likes to hear that! In fact, we tend to freak out, because we make a giant leap: Our friend is nearing death! In our modern Western culture we generally don't like to acknowledge death, talk about it, or plan for it. That's too bad, because if we overcome that hurdle, we can better navigate the important — and sometimes wonderfully long — phase before death: seniorhood! Keep in mind, being classified as a senior hardly means that the end of life is looming. What it does mean is that it's time to keep a closer eye and to offer a bit more help. Just like for our aging human family members, regular life feels a little harder as a body gets older, and it sure is nice when loved ones ease that burden.

This chapter of the book is about how to navigate the senior phase of your dog's life with nuanced understanding and grace. Rather than denying you've arrived there, you can choose to step up. You can recognize where your dog no longer has full function and arrange things so that both you and your dog can enjoy this phase of the journey.

Help Your Dog Age Well

Let's start with what we can do to extend good health as long as possible. Just as a human who's been eating sensibly and doing yoga for a decade will almost certainly retain mobility longer than a smoker who's a couch potato, not all dogs have the same shot at aging well. To increase the odds that your dog will be one who seems very much herself until a ripe old age, focus on the following things.

Exercise

First, think about appropriate exercise. The phrase "motion is lotion" is as true for dogs as it is for humans. The key, though, is providing and encouraging the *right* kind of motion. While you don't want to let your middle-aged dog just nap on the sofa day after day, you also don't want to drag her on hikes that leave her sore. Enter our hero: the gentle twice-a-day stroll at your dog's chosen pace. Is it two miles or just up to the next house? Nobody can tell you except your own dog. Pay attention to body language during a walk; encourage, but never force; and watch for stiffness or soreness a day afterward. Above all, avoid the dreaded weekend warrior concept: no activity for a week and then big hikes on Saturday and Sunday. Instead, make a point of building in the right level of movement every day to sustain muscle mass and keep potentially arthritic dogs feeling their best. Plus, let the walk be what we call a "sniffari": Allow your dog to take her time and sniff to her heart's content. Unbridled sniffing offers the brain-enrichment equivalent of old people doing the crossword to fend off memory loss.

Nutrition

Second, keep an eye on your dog's diet. It is incredibly easy to spoil an old friend with cookies and bully sticks.

But to help him be at his best to face the ticking life clock, you want to keep your dog's body at the right weight and fueled by powerful nutrients. No, we're not going to tell you to deprive your best friend of treats. Instead, embrace the idea of thinking small: We know you love to give him that large Milk-Bone. But guess what? With a teeny, tiny smear of cream cheese on the end of your finger, you can create the same gleeful moment that surprises and delights your friend. Or reach into the freezer and make a big deal of a frozen green bean. Then give ten more, one at a time, turning it into a game. Engagement and connection without a health downside is a win-win.

Stress Reduction

This one is easily missed. Pay attention to stress, which can exacerbate most health concerns. Think your dog doesn't have any stress? Maybe. But it's also possible that her days are filled with things she *used to* enjoy but that have now become sources of concern or discomfort. For example, it is natural for dogs who adored the dog park to have very little interest in play with other dogs as they age. Dogs who used to like nothing more than greeting all the strangers on a walk down Main Street may begin to shy away from outstretched hands. Dogs who used to be at their very best in the middle of a second grader's birthday party can start to find kid chaos overwhelming. It is incredibly easy not to notice this change in enthusiasms, because your dog has been a certain way for years and years. But if you've missed it, you may be regularly putting your dog into situations she now finds stressful. The answer is simply to pay attention to body language. Be ready for your dog to find some things (such as crowds, strangers, guests, or noises) newly stressful.

When you see reluctance, offer a better alternative, like some cozy, enjoyable downtime at home. Chewing is a natural de-stressor for dogs, so hand over a rubber food toy like a Toppl or a Kong. Stuff it with a nutritious mixture, perhaps your dog's regular kibble stirred into plain yogurt and plain pumpkin, then add a smear of peanut butter on top. The first few times, you'll want to give her a fresh, aromatic version, but once your dog gets the hang of this toy, you can try freezing it to make it into a longer-lasting activity.

Weekly At-Home Exams

Make a weekly date to gently examine your dog's entire body. All sorts of potential evils are no big deal if caught in time but are quite painful if not dealt with early. Create a Sunday-night ritual as you sit in front of the TV. Keep your basket of brushes, clippers, and ear wipes right there. Establish a pattern where you give your dog a nice massage so he relaxes into this process. This is your chance to catch lumps and skin infections right at the start. And if your dog's coat is longish, find a way to do some brushing even if you have to do it in three-second bursts. Lots of aging pets come to the vet very matted, and their loving owners say they just don't want to upset them by brushing. That's valid — see "Stress Reduction" above — but if you create a weekly routine, those mats never have a chance to get started. Big mats hurt because they pull on the skin. Ear infections are awful. Long nails make walking painful and more slippery. Down the road, there may be things you can't do anything about, but these? You can make these "problems" disappear with just a little commitment, and this can make a dramatic difference in your dog's comfort and health.

Vet Visits

Finally, think about increasing your dog's wellness vet appointments to twice a year, and consider checking bloodwork every time. It may seem expensive when that panel turns up with no issues, but when it catches something serious-but-treatable early — kidney disease, liver dysfunction, thyroid disease — it'll be worth every penny. (If you are in the financial position to play it super safe, or if you have terrific pet insurance, you could add annual chest X-rays and abdominal ultrasounds, which would help your vet detect trends and tumors that aren't palpable.)

Look for Signs of Aging

While there is no one-size-fits-all description of canine aging, some changes are very common, though they hit individual dogs with various levels of severity and speed. These are the things you'll want to look out for:

- Difficulty with mobility and navigation
- Vision loss
- Hearing loss
- Change in elimination habits (as their systems slow down, older dogs may experience more constipation, incontinence, and/or a greater vulnerability to urinary tract infections)

- Change in eating habits (aging dogs sometimes experience a decreased appetite and appear to be more finicky about food, resulting in weight loss)
- Change in sleeping habits
- Decrease in stamina for activities
- Lowered tolerance for all sorts of things: heat, other dogs, young kids, and so on
- Increased anxiety
- Cognitive decline or confusion
- Visible physical changes
  - Muscle atrophy
  - Dulling or changing of the coat
  - Bad breath
  - Cloudy eyes
  - Lumps and bumps

These changes can take place so slowly you don't realize anything has happened, until one day you notice your dog unable to get up from the tiled floor or not responding when you call her name because she can't hear you.

The biggest thing you can do for your old friend: Take note of changes. The earlier you spot things, the earlier you can assist your dog and minimize the trouble.

Adjust Your Home Environment Continually

While there's sometimes not much you (or your vet) can do to address a certain issue — like declining mobility or eyesight — in many cases you can make simple changes to minimize the impact that issue has on your dog's life. You can set up your home environment so that it continues to be a place he can navigate well. It's crucial throughout seniorhood to be as proactive as possible, looking to make small adjustments as needed.

Think about the changes we see in elderly people's homes: extra handrails, a ramp, a pull-down seat in the shower, and so on. Those things help folks stay in their homes longer, feeling safe and capable. We can make similar environmental changes to support our dogs. Not only will that help keep them safer physically — if they're already having trouble going down steps, it certainly won't help if they then fall down a flight of stairs! — but it will also help address one of the more ignored sadnesses of old age: increased anxiety. Whether you're a human or a dog, losing function makes you feel less secure.

The fact that your dog's condition may vary day to day — three good days in a row, then one bad one — doesn't mean you should hold off on making the home safer and easier for him. All sorts of things can affect how your dog is feeling and how cooperative his body seems to be: the weather, how active he was the day before, and how much he ate at breakfast. As they age, our dogs don't bounce back as easily as they did before, and it can be just as upsetting to them as it is to us. So once you notice a diminishing ability, simply plan for it rather than turning a blind eye and only "seeing" the good days.

After all these easy years of having an adult in his prime with no need for special accommodations, it can feel daunting to realize you may now be carefully managing the environment again — much like you did during puppyhood. But don't despair! In the long run, setting things up to cater to your changing dog will ease so much stress for you both. Read on for some easy-to-implement ideas.

Add Nonslip Flooring

Have you ever tried walking across ice in shoes with no grip? Or across wooden floors in slippery socks? It's unnerving, right? You're suddenly not in control of your body because the surface you are on feels unstable and the environment unpredictable. Senior dogs feel this way a lot because of arthritis, decreasing muscle tone, and other joint/mobility issues. If you look closely, you'll often see an older dog trying to avoid surfaces that now feel slippery (even though a year ago they didn't) and sometimes opting simply to stay in a different room rather than cross the scary kitchen.

When you see changing behavior in your senior, get in the habit of wondering why it's happening. In a surprising percentage of cases, it's because that dog feels a lot of anxiety about walking across a particular surface. This is one of the good problems because it is so easy to fix.

At first, you may just need a few rugs in key spots that work like safety islands helping your senior get a grip as she moves through her day. Folks are often shocked when they see the utter transformation in their senior dogs as soon as that slip-free path is in place. Their dogs are suddenly more relaxed and active than they've been in a long time.

As for what to use, pick something cheap so that you feel generous about scattering all sorts of them around your house! Your local home goods store will have rubber-backed runners, and online you can get all kinds of washable slip-proof rugs in a variety of sizes. Even yoga mats work in a pinch.

As time goes on, you may need to up your game and cover a great deal more of the house. The key spots to worry about are:

- the main pathway
- areas of transition, like the entrance from outside or the bottom of a step
- places where the dog may lie down and then try to get up
- areas where the dog eats and drinks

In addition, if you have multiple dogs in the home (or a new puppy who may be boisterous and overly excited), areas of coexistence should definitely have nonslip flooring so the older dog can safely communicate and either engage or leave interactions without being knocked over or feeling extra vulnerable.

Think About One-Level Living

Stairs are often the first indicators that a dog has begun to struggle with mobility. The dog who used to fly up and down entire staircases in play is now hesitating before taking a first step.

In the beginning, there's a bit you can do to help keep full access to the house for your dog. First, make sure all stairs have great grip. Even dogs in their prime feel uncomfortable on bare wood staircases! If you don't want to install carpet, you can get rubber-backed stair pads that can help a lot.

The next step is to minimize the reasons the dog might feel pushed to do the stairs, and to show up to help when those times do occur. Each trip up and down may be more wear and tear for that aging body, and it may add to the anxiety the dog feels about not being as strong as he used to be. So maybe you block off the stairs for much of the day, and then you all go up together at night.

At some point, most seniors do lose the ability to navigate a full staircase. It's a great idea to take a few moments while your dog's still in great shape to ponder what you're going to do about that. If you happen to use your second floor a lot — maybe you have a home office there and your dog is always at your feet, and at night the dog sleeps up there in bed with you — you might consider finding ways to develop more downstairs together time. Just like retirees sometimes start looking for a one-level home "just in case," it's smart to think about how life would look if your dog couldn't follow you upstairs. Do you have a cozy hangout space downstairs?

If you have a smaller dog, or better upper-body strength than this book's authors do, carrying your old dog up and down the stairs to bed or outside can be an option at first. However, consider what may happen if lifting and setting down your dog becomes painful or scary for him. While carrying can work in many cases, it's not always the best long-term solution. It's good to have a one-level living option available just in case.

Consider a "Senior Space"

Eventually, slowly but surely, making one change at a time, you may end up creating a "senior space" that has no stairs at all. You'll set your old friend up in a nice spot where everything's in easy reach — food and water, bed, potty area, and calm activities like chewing or sunbathing — and nothing produces anxiety. Bonus points if there's a couch in there where you can sleep if you feel like joining her sometimes!

For some, the idea of a senior space of confinement and limited access sounds sad. They're used to their younger, athletic dogs who've been romping through the house with ease for years. It seems mean to cut that off.

But in fact, it's the opposite. Often, designing a senior space well gives the dog an obvious increase in peace of mind. As our dogs get older, more arthritic, and even incontinent, they experience a lot of stress in a too-big environment. For example, they suddenly know they need the potty area, but — ack — they can't get their body to move fast enough anymore! Giving a senior easy and close access to her key resources (food, water, bed, potty area) is a wonderful way to lower anxiety and help her feel more herself.

A senior space is especially key if the dog spends considerable time at home while her people are at work. At the opposite end of the spectrum, a senior space can keep an older dog safe when the house is too filled with busy people who might not always be looking where they're going: Senior dogs are less able to scamper out of the way and can easily be stepped on or tripped over if not protected.

Sometimes when folks consider where to create this space, they decide they have the perfect spot — let's say the back hallway by the garage. As nice as it might feel to compartmentalize the dog mess that way, your sweet old friend still wants to be included. Her space needs to be in an area of the house that she's familiar with, where she won't be isolated from the daily activities of the home, and where she will feel safe and secure. Many people gate off a corner of their main living room to create an inclusive senior space.

Keep in mind that the dog doesn't have to be in the senior space all the time. Some seniors will be able to hang out in the rest of the house when a family member is home to supervise. However, having a safe senior space allows for peace of mind when you can't keep an eye. Taking the time to start acclimating your older dog to spending time in this space sooner rather than later will make it a positive place and reduce overall anxiety.

Shift Sleeping Arrangements and Cuddle Time

One of the hardest transitions for senior dogs *and* their caretakers is when declining mobility affects cuddle time. Maybe the dog is no longer able to follow them upstairs to bed to sleep with them or no longer able to jump on the sofa or chairs to snuggle. All kinds of ramps and short stairs are available, but those can create a new problem: What about getting down? Dogs with decreasing muscle tone, balance issues, or impaired eyesight can fall off and injure themselves.

One solution: Start sitting on the floor with them instead of the sofa. Create a cozy cuddle spot on the carpet rather than the couch. Just as you do with the senior space, you may need to gradually transition your dog to this new arrangement.

The same goes with sleeping. The senior space may be in an area of the house that now means you are sleeping apart for the first time, and while this may be better logistically — especially if your senior dog is dealing with incontinence — it may be very hard for you both emotionally. Some great options for the senior space include air mattresses, floor futons, even a low-to-the-ground sleeper sofa. These allow you to transition your dog slowly without leaving him alone and also lend a comforting option for a possible end-of-life phase when you don't want to be more than a few feet apart.

Manage Incontinence

If you've suddenly noticed your old dog having more accidents than she used to, she may be losing control of her bladder and/or bowels. This is a normal part of aging that happens to many dogs during their senior years. It can evolve gradually — one accident here and there to start — or kick in suddenly and persistently. Either way, it can be very distressing for your old dog (and you). Most dogs are extremely clean by nature, and you can see how upsetting this new state of affairs feels to them. As frustrating (and let's be honest, gross) as it can be sometimes, it's important to remember that this is not a voluntary change and is simply part of the aging process.

Incontinence can take different forms, and usually it doesn't mean complete lack of control. Typically it starts with a dog no longer being able to hold her bladder or bowels for the same length of time anymore. Of course, you'll want to check with the vet to rule out medical issues like a urinary tract infection (UTI), but usually the dog's muscular function is simply not as strong as it once was. In other cases, she may be dealing with some cognitive degeneration to the point that she forgets what the process of "asking" to go out looks like, and by the time she figures it out, she's already had an accident.

The incontinence phase is nobody's favorite time. If you're lucky, the most you'll need to do is just be more aware: Take your dog out more frequently (every couple of hours), and limit access to carpeted areas. However, at some point you may find yourself dealing with frequent indoor elimination. You'll want to be assessing quality of life as your dog declines in this way, but in the meantime, here are some pointers to make this stage feel less challenging:

- **Set out pee pads.** If you do this, your dog will likely start to use them instead of the bare floor. Washable pee pads are often a much better option than disposable ones. They are incredibly absorbent, easy to pop in the washer, and come in many sizes. They also provide a nonslip surface for your aging dog, so they multitask in a way the disposable ones do not.

- **Set up a cleaning station.** Have paper towels, tissues, poop bags, spray cleaner and/or antibacterial wipes for the floor, and a trash receptacle ready so you can quickly take care of any messes. You may become very practiced in the environmentally friendly skill of using only a tissue to pick up a stray poop that you can then pop right in the toilet! A package of pet-safe, skin-safe wipes comes in handy for dogs who are left with a messy bum after a poop or who accidentally lie in a mess or drag a paw through it.

- **Use doggy diapers and belly bands sparingly.** Diapers and belly bands (essentially urine-containing diapers for males that wrap around the belly) offer the obvious advantage of keeping a house cleaner. However, they're usually harder on our dogs, who don't like the feeling of being trapped in their own waste and can develop a UTI or what's essentially diaper rash. Setting up a senior space with pee pads always available is a better all-around choice, but doggy diapers and belly bands can be a great solution for certain times when you want your dog to be able to have the run of the house or when, say, you bring your senior over to your sister's place for a visit.

Ease the Anxiety of Change

It's awful to feel like you can't do something physically anymore even though mentally you still feel capable. We see this frustration often in old dogs. They may try to jump up on the couch like they used to, but now find they fall. They may be on their way out to eliminate and discover it's already happening. It sounds like anthropomorphizing, but it's fairly clear they feel hurt and humiliation. This is part of the reason we see increased anxiety in senior dogs, and as your dog's friend and caretaker, you can play a giant role in easing that psychological discomfort.

- **Don't ignore the change.** Once you see your dog struggling with a task he once found easy, immediately strategize ways to help him accomplish his goal. For example, if you see your dog start trying to jump in the car a few times before actually making it, get a ramp immediately.

- **Don't encourage him to keep trying.** Our well-intentioned encouragement can often nudge elderly dogs to push through pain and potentially injure themselves because they don't want to miss out. If your dog is struggling with climbing the stairs at night, don't keep calling him up. That will only make him more anxious.

- **Do support the new limits,** and help your older dog feel comfort in them. Change can be scary, but if you guide your dog through it and work together with him, as a team, it's a lot less worrying for your dog. New ramp for the car? Okay, let's try this together! Can't make it to the door for potty breaks every time? That's okay — here's a new potty space inside.

- **Do give options.** Can't jump up on the couch anymore? Here are three new beds to choose from: one at my feet, one by the fireplace, and one in the other room. Variety and choice help many aging dogs feel like they still have autonomy and are not powerless in this change. After a couple of days, they may even realize they prefer the new bed to the couch!

Aging is often more stressful for our dogs than it needs to be. Your acceptance and support make a huge difference in their ability to cope and feel at ease with their new parameters and needs. The sooner we start helping them adjust, the easier it is on both human and canine.

Get on a First-Name Basis with Your Vet(s)

If you're lucky, your dog's adult life has mostly featured yearly wellness vet visits, plus the odd appointment for an ear infection, allergic reaction, or broken dewclaw. That typically changes in the senior phase, when — just like with humans — it's key to touch base with medical professionals more often to keep your dog comfortable and stay ahead of any developing issues. It helps to understand that this is part of the process, and to plan for it, so that you're not thrown for a loop (emotionally *and* financially) every time.

Having a good relationship with your veterinarian can greatly ease the challenges of the senior phase. Your vet can help you understand what to watch for over the years and help you catch any pain, stress, or discomfort early. In this trickier stage of your dog's life, you're particularly going to want to be able to rely on the guidance of a vet you trust who is easy to talk to. If you don't feel comfortable with your vet, it'll be hard to work effectively with them to find the right path regarding meds, therapies, diet changes, lifestyle hacks, and possible procedures to keep your dog feeling as good as she can for as long as she can. If you don't feel particularly good about anyone at your vet clinic, perhaps it's time to look around for a new vet before you have serious issues? Ideally, you'll have not just one vet you like but even a backup favorite, since yours won't always be available. It's hard to turn to a stranger in a stressful medical moment.

Keep in mind that, even if you adore your own vet, you may have the dreaded 3 a.m. emergency when they're unavailable. Emergency vet clinics are usually open 24-7, and while hopefully you'll never need to use one, knowing ahead of time where your nearest one is and how they handle new clients will make a difference when it counts.

Be a Well-Prepared Vet Client

Over time and lots of animals, the two of us have learned that the success of the vet relationship largely lies in our own hands. There is a client and a vet in every appointment, and it makes a significant difference if both of you are well prepared. While this is always true, it may be even more important during senior care when eventually you'll be having end-of-life discussions.

Just as we dog owners want vets who are easy to talk to, our vets want clients they can be honest with. You can't get the best advice if you're in denial. You can't make the best choices if you haven't been listening closely, asking good questions, and linking the doctor's comments with what you've observed at home.

To be an effective advocate for your senior dog, you'll want to be ready to present a very clear idea of what's been happening day to day, even if the changes have been subtle. Remember that if you don't speak up, the vet has no choice but to base her recommendations on only what she sees in front of her, and often symptoms magically disappear the second you step into the clinic. Some veterinarians are conservative with pain management, so it can be incredibly helpful to bring in a video of how your dog moves after a long walk or behaves at dinnertime (now lying down or chewing slowly). The seemingly small things you observe at home may help your vet know where care needs to be directed.

As your dog declines, you may begin to face quality-of-life and end-of-life discussions. This can be very difficult, particularly if you've never been in this position before. Try to do your part to set the stage for the best possible care by being totally transparent and asking your vet to speak candidly. Do you need support — and two sets of ears — during those appointments? If so, can you have your partner or a friend come with you to help ask good questions and get all the clarification you need?

The vet industry is stretched thin these days, and when things get very serious, it may be a good idea to book a double appointment to be sure you have the time you need to talk through very hard choices. Some vets now have external resources and support systems, such as companion-animal end-of-life doulas or hospice-certified technicians, so be sure to take advantage of those if they could help you. Ideally, you'll be able to develop a plan for what your wishes are should your best friend decline very quickly.

No discussion of veterinary care is complete without an acknowledgment of the financial implications. While not all dogs end up requiring expensive intervention in their twilight, many do. It can be a shock if you haven't planned for it. Veterinary costs are currently at all-time highs because of a perfect storm: incredible canine medical advancement (we can fix so much that we couldn't before); corporate consolidation; a shortage of vets and vet techs; and the fallout from the pandemic pet boom. You'll have less stress and extra options on the table if you either (a) put savings aside for senior care or (b) carefully research and sign up for pet insurance. (As with human health insurance, premiums are higher for those more likely to need care, so older pets are more expensive to insure. Depending on the plan, signing up early while your dog is not yet elderly can help.)

Learn About Pain Management

Think of the people you know who are in their seventies and eighties. What do they talk about all the time? Aches and pains! "Oh, my bursitis today…" It's no different for our dogs as their bodies age — except in their case they can't talk to us about exactly where it hurts. Because of that, lots of deeply loved older dogs are enduring pain they don't need to, every day. If their owners actually knew how their dogs felt, they'd want to address it immediately, but signs of canine pain are so easy for us humans to miss!

So when you think about how you want to pamper and spoil your sweet old pooch, think first about the loving gift of close observation. Watch carefully for changes — moving differently, avoiding things, acting cranky, no longer jumping up on the couch, having less tolerance for movement/chaos/noise — and discuss them with your vet.

Sometimes owners put off giving their elderly dogs pain medication because they are concerned about side effects. We hope you'll voice that concern to your vet so that they can talk it through with you. Many dogs never experience side effects at all. For others, there may be a mild change. For example, a med might make a dog a bit sleepier, but it's well worth the extra, pain-free bounce in his step when awake. In other cases, a drug may have side effects once a dog has been on it for quite some time, but that is simply not a worry for our beloved seniors. In short, there's no way to know how a certain pain management approach is going to affect your particular dog until you try.

A key philosophy to adopt for seniors is that medical care is always about getting a higher quality of life. It's not about gaining more time but making the most of the time they have. Most of us who've had the chance to observe many dogs throughout their later stages have the very strong feeling that they'd rather have six months pain-free and able to do all the things that bring them joy than eighteen months of pain and limitations. Experienced owners almost always explore the options for pain relief earlier rather than later because they've learned how much happier their dog can feel.

To get more comfortable with pain med usage, don't be shy about asking your vet to walk you through the options. A wide variety of drugs is available now, backed by lots of studies to build confidence in their usage. Some can be given on an as-needed basis; others must build up in the system to be effective. Some require regular bloodwork, which is yet another reason not to worry about side effects because testing will show if there's an issue.

Keep in mind too the various nonmedication options: acupuncture, laser therapy, and physical therapy. Ask about them! They can work in tandem with meds.

Don't be surprised if you see an immediate improvement in your dog's behavior, movement, and overall attitude when you start a pain relief program! It's a wonderful thing to witness. That said, if an old dog has lived with chronic pain for a long time, it may take longer to see behavioral change. They may still behave in anticipation of certain movements or behaviors causing pain, and it isn't until they have been on the medication for a while that they begin to relax.

Weigh the Risks of Procedures

As your dog ages, there's good reason to worry a bit more about procedures that require sedation or anesthesia — things that an aging body doesn't tolerate as well or bounce back from as easily.

Vets recommend many procedures for senior dog wellness. Dental cleanings, lump removals, and biopsies are just some of the possible interventions that may be on the table. While in earlier years all of those might have been an automatic "yes," for senior dogs it may be time to weigh the benefits versus the risks of sedation, anesthesia, and recovery time. In the beginning stages of aging, a simple lump removal may not be a big deal, but later on it might result in a difficult recovery. Is it worth it? How much time is left? What are the implications if the issue is left alone?

Ideally, you'll feel comfortable fully discussing all this with your vet and considering together your dog's history and stress level. Ask if there are any other ways to treat the issue that don't involve sedation/anesthesia.

Remember that it's okay to decline to treat something if that aligns with your overall goal of valuing quality of life over length of life. Many vets will wholeheartedly support a decision to skip a particular procedure in order to make the most of your time with your best friend.

Assess Quality of Life

Once you realize that your dog is entering her senior period of life, consider keeping a diary to assess wellness. Whether it's on your phone, on your computer, or in a notebook, keep track of how your dog is doing. You might initially start on a monthly or biweekly basis and as your assessments begin to show a steady decline, increase the frequency to weekly or even daily. Staying consistent about what you're recording and how you're presenting this information can help you and your vet determine what the next steps may be, whether that's pain management, more testing, or end-of-life discussions.

Observing a senior dog well can be challenging. Older dogs are mostly declining in their abilities, and because this process can stretch over a period of months or years, it can be difficult to discern what's a new change and what's been going on for a while. It helps to use three key elements to track change and determine quality of life in senior dogs: function, purpose, and joy.

Function

Assessing function means tracking the basics: the body's physical ability to interact normally with its environment, diet, and patterns of living. We want to see a dog eat, move, sleep, and eliminate with the least disruption. To make it easier to prompt good observations, you can break function into categories. These are the primary ones:

- **Moving.** Is my dog walking and moving well, or is that function being impeded by disease, age, the environment, or all three? Are ease and amount of movement declining over time?
- **Eating.** Is my dog eating and drinking normally, or is that increasing or decreasing?

- **Sleeping.** Is my dog getting adequate quality sleep? (Note that an interruption or decrease in sleep can result in the decline of other functions — as anyone who has had a newborn baby knows!)
- **Eliminating.** Is my dog having more accidents? If so, are they pee or poop or both?
- **Eyesight, hearing, and alertness.** Have I seen anything out of the ordinary happen that might suggest my dog's had a decrease in ability or alertness — perhaps not noticing when someone enters the home or barking at the sight of something that shouldn't be worrisome.

Make a point of tracking each category, because the clearer your sense of what's really going on, the better your odds of finding an intervention that helps. You may find that a drop-off in one function is driving a decline in another. For example, a dog who can't walk well may eat less because the bowl feels far away — so adding nonslip rugs could well improve movement *and* suddenly help your dog polish off his meals.

As another instance of crossover function loss, if your dog is experiencing cognitive decline, it may disrupt his ability to sleep well. Or pain can interfere with good sleep, which ends up creating the appearance of cognitive decline! Feel confused? Brainstorm with your vet. You may be able to come up with adjustments that help a great deal to slow declines in function.

Purpose

While physical function is important, it's not the only way we measure an animal's quality of life. Like us, dogs

Supporting Your Senior

need to feel a sense of purpose in order to thrive and enjoy their days.

Having trouble picturing the concept of canine purpose? Think about a dog barking an intruder off the porch (okay, it was really just the Amazon guy), and you'll know what we mean. It's something that the dog feels a need or a drive to do. It may be genetic (think herding), or it might be their own history (a learned love of obedience/agility/trick training), or it might just be their individual personality (giving companionship). No matter what, though, their purpose is something that brings meaning and enjoyment into their life.

Senior dogs, even as their physical function declines, are still more than capable of having purpose. It may shift or lessen in intensity as they age, but we don't want to see it gone completely. Let's say your dog chased squirrels relentlessly in her younger years but now barely lifts her head when one crosses directly in front of her. That's something to pay attention to, because that dog is definitely declining in her sense of purpose.

Sometimes, though, declining function inhibits purpose. If the dog has lost eyesight or hearing and now can no longer react to stimuli the same way, that is not the purpose itself declining, but the function affecting it. Happy senior dogs (with attentive owners who'll help problem-solve) can sometimes find another way to fulfill that purpose. For example, let's say you have a Jack Russell terrier who has always loved to dig in the yard, but as she loses strength and balance, she's not quite able to do that. You might find that putting a pile of small fluffy blankets in the family room that she can happily dig into gives her an easy way to continue to exercise that drive. It's wonderful when a substitute like that does the trick, but if it does not, that's crucial to track because quality of life will become affected.

Joy

Lastly, there's joy. Joy and purpose often overlap for dogs, but they're not the same. For example, the dog who likes to chase squirrels as a purpose may experience joy from sunbathing on the couch when the sun shines through the window. Dogs who love to do obedience training as a purpose may find joy in chewing a bone by the woodstove in the evening. What gives your dog joy? As a senior, how often does he still feel that?

Cognitive decline typically results in loss of joy for many senior dogs, even if they are physically functioning well. As they start getting lost, anxious, or increasingly disoriented, they may have a hard time finding the same joy they did when they were younger. This is often one of the hardest things to witness as a senior dog caretaker, because although the body is functioning well, the mind has lost the ability to give the dog joy, and that is a defining criterion for assessing quality of life.

Quality-of-Life Questionnaire

Below is a questionnaire Helen created for her clients to use in the wellness diaries she encourages them to keep. Of course, there are lots of detailed, complex checklists on the internet designed to help assess your dog's quality of life. Most of them ask you to assign a numerical score to each area of potential decline, resulting in a final tally that purports to give you a solid answer on just what stage your dog may have reached. The problem with this is that it gives the impression of a scientific basis to something that is more of a gut call. That can be misleading. This simple form is more helpful, because it loosely guides you to think through the key factors — and doing that regularly turns you into a skilled observer of the meaningful changes in your dog.

Senior Dog Quality-of-Life Questionnaire

Did your dog have good function today…	YES	NO	MAYBE	COMMENTS
moving?				
eating?				
sleeping?				
eliminating?				
seeing, hearing, and being alert?				

Dogs find meaning in different things: guarding the home, offering companionship, chasing off intruders, digging for vermin, working with their human (training), etc.

Did your dog have purpose today?
❑ YES ❑ NO ❑ MAYBE

What activities give your dog a sense of purpose?

Did your dog have joy today?
❑ YES ❑ NO ❑ MAYBE

What brings your dog joy? Is it playing with a ball? Lying in the sun? Chewing a bone? Snuggling with you?

Did pain or disease interfere today?
❑ YES ❑ NO ❑ MAYBE

Is pain or disease affecting function, purpose, or joy? Are your methods of dealing with disease and pain helping? Are any of those methods themselves interfering with function, purpose, or joy?

Last question: How are you feeling about your dog's life today?

_____

Function, purpose, and joy. Our dogs need all three to have a good quality of life. As they age, the greatest gift we can give them is to observe them closely and then adjust things accordingly to help them. Inevitably, though, at some point our ability to boost that function-purpose-joy quotient is not enough. Then it's time to think about how to give the final gift: the best goodbye possible (we'll guide you through this in chapter 5: "Savoring the Sunset").

Chapter Two

Welcoming a Puppy

When we notice our beloved dog aging, it's natural to think about getting a puppy. We love the idea of a new pup being influenced by our dear old friend, and it sounds comforting to have a furry family member around to soften the inevitable loss. However, after many years with a great dog, it's easy to lose sight of just how all-consuming puppyhood is! The more informed you are about what it takes to raise a puppy, the better positioned you'll be.

Just the thought of a new puppy is enough to lift the spirits: that face, the snuggles, the antics, the laughter in the room. Add to that the promise of a deep friendship to come, and few things in life can summon joy the way a puppy can.

Even with all that, though, caring for puppies around the clock can be a shock. Who knew you could have so many urgent questions in one day? Of course, advice is coming at you from every direction — with websites, podcasts, and social media always at your fingertips — but frankly that's a recipe for paralysis. It's too much.

Taking a cue from the appliance manufacturers, here is our version of a "quick-start guide" to a puppy. If you're on the fence about whether adding a puppy is right for you at the moment, this chapter will give you a sense of what it's like to have an adorable little life-upender in the house. And if that sweet new baby is already snuggling in your lap, this overview will help you navigate the first weeks. (See chapter 3 for details on how to manage puppyhood while you have a senior too.)

Because this is just a quick-start guide, it's bound to prompt more in-depth questions as we touch on various topics. We can't cover it all here, but you'll find much more detail in Kathy's full-length book on puppyhood, *Welcoming Your Puppy from Planet Dog*.

Ease the Puppy's Transition

Bringing a puppy home is so exciting — for the humans! But keep in mind that it can be a tough transition for the little one. Remember, even though you've been eagerly anticipating adding her to your family, she had no idea this was going to happen. In fact, she may feel she's been kidnapped from Planet Dog, where she spent all her time happily playing, wrestling, and snuggling with her littermates. Now she's in a mysterious land filled with humans and their different rules! Take heart, though: An approach guided by empathy will ease that transition and help her feel safe here on Planet Human.

If you can, schedule the puppy's arrival for when you

can be fully home a few days in a row to help her settle in. Your soothing, playful presence will help her feel she's going to be okay here. You'll want to be as calm and consistent as possible, making her new world feel predictable and full of good things. The first week is the time to establish the most important concept of all: trust. She needs to know she can count on you.

A key part of building that trust is to be sensitive regarding body handling. While many pups seek out cuddles, most like to have a choice in the matter regarding when, how, and by whom they are touched. As hard as it is to resist picking up and hugging a puppy, giving her agency is essential. Let her choose you. If pup is leaning away or squirming when you try to hold her, find a different way to engage: Get on the floor and give a play bow, dangle a toy, or toss a treat. The eventual snuggle is all the sweeter when it's mutual.

Create a "Puppy Apartment"

As soon as they get home, puppies begin to do what comes naturally to those from Planet Dog — jumping, chewing, mouthing, digging. That's why one of the smartest puppyhood moves you can make is to immediately get your setup working for you. If you put only good choices in front of your puppy, you'll be able to reward lots of great behavior, offering a shining path to what works out happily for him here. (It also steers you away from the dynamic where days are filled with the word *no*, which is unpleasant for you, unfair to the pup, and a setback for the new relationship between you.)

So how do you create a good setup? Keep in mind that puppies pee, poop, and chew. Constantly. So save them, save your stuff, and save your sanity by limiting all of that to one area for the first month or two. Whatever you do, do not let a new puppy have the run of the house. Instead, create a smaller "puppy apartment": a puppy-proofed room or section of a room that serves as the youngster's main living space. This might be your kitchen or your family room with the rugs rolled up and lower knickknacks cleared away. Soon enough, you can add another room, then another. In the beginning, you'll want to set it up to have:

- easy access to the outdoors for potty training
- no carpet that can hold on to scent
- a pen and/or crate, because more levels of management are always helpful
- enough space and furnishings for you to happily hang out in it a lot

Note what the puppy apartment is *not*: It is not just a pen, nor is it an isolated bedroom, basement, or laundry room. Those setups don't work well because the pup doesn't want to be alone, and after the initial honeymoon days, the humans don't want to hang out in those tiny spaces. Result? Either a crying puppy or one who's constantly taken out of that area into the big, non-puppy-proofed areas. Ack! Instead, you want a safe space where the puppy can hang out *with you*, be a part of the household routine, and learn to settle around you — rather than viewing your presence as a big, exciting occasion deserving of all sorts of jumping and mouthing.

To create that puppy apartment, you will likely need

to buy or borrow some baby gates or wire-panel x-pens to block doorways and close off space. Sure, that equipment can be ugly, but so is your mood when your carpet is ruined and your new shoes destroyed. (Actually, these days you can find gorgeous stand-up room dividers with easy swing gates that you won't hate!) Bottom line: Set up your pup for success by (1) limiting his ability to do things we deem undesirable here on Planet Human, and (2) giving him a chance to live right alongside you, where it's easy for you to notice and reward what you *do* want to see. A thoughtfully designed puppy apartment allows you to do both.

As for the rest of the house, those rooms are for fun, world-expanding, confidence-building supervised field trips. If your pup has just gone to the bathroom outside, you have a short window of time for an accident-free indoor adventure. Have him experience story time in your kid's room, music in your bedroom, and the sound of the dryer in the laundry room. Then it's back to the puppy apartment.

Fully Commit to Potty Training

When it comes to potty training, if you focus 100 percent for the first month, you can be pretty much done. If you're mellow and inconsistent at this stage, you may still have a confused dog peeing and pooping in your house a year from now. So let's buckle up and get it over with!

> **Rule #1: Somebody *always* has an eye on the pup unless she's in the crate.** This approach virtually eliminates mistakes, which is the key to speedy training. (Unfortunately for us all, "eye on" does

not mean "in same room with laptop open.") When you're observing carefully, you'll recognize when your pup is about to go — maybe she suddenly stops playing and heads for a particular corner, sniffing — and that's when you cheerily scoop her up, take her outside, and tell her what a "good girl!" she is after she goes.

It's easy to get lax and think one little puddle in the kitchen doesn't matter, and you'd rather clean that up later than take her out *yet again*. Alas, that puddle is more than a little cleanup job. It's a predictor that potty training will take longer now.

Larger households may benefit from an official system designating who's on duty when. If Mom, Dad, and kids are all sitting around together, it's easy to think somebody else is paying attention. Try passing around an "I'm on potty duty" lanyard every hour!

Rule #2: At first, take the pup outside every half hour (unless she's asleep). If you're having zero accidents (and only if you're having zero accidents) move to every forty-five minutes and then every hour. Accident? Go back to every half hour. We know: You can't believe it has to be that often. But taking puppies out before they really must go prevents mistakes. Every time your puppy pees outdoors, it's cementing the idea that that's where this event takes place. The reverse happens too: Every time she pees inside, she is learning it's okay to pee inside, not to mention leaving a hard-to-remove scent marker that virtually guarantees her body will later respond by eliminating in that exact spot.

Rule #3: Walk outside with the pup, every time. If you simply open the door, the pup will likely choose not to go out — and then pee in your kitchen two seconds later. We need to put on our shoes and get out there. Even in the rain. Even when we're tired. Even when we're on the phone. The motion of walking, and the smell of pee in the grass, makes them "go" — and that gives us an opportunity to praise them. The more that happens, the faster the puppy learns.

And yes, you can add a treat into this process, which sometimes brings extra clarity to the teaching. But be careful to wait until your pup is truly finished eliminating to celebrate. Some pups cut their stream of pee short because their human is about to exuberantly reward them, so it's a great practice to wait a beat. While they're still "going," don't talk or make eye contact. Wait until they finish on their own and start walking to begin the party.

If you're doing it right, potty training is absolutely exhausting. Great job if that's how you feel! That means you'll be done before you know it.

Be Prepared for Those Teeth

Puppies explore the world with their mouths, and unprepared humans come away with the little bite marks to prove it. The best way to deal with sharp puppy teeth is not to be surprised by them. Arm yourself with an endless supply of legal outlets for that natural impulse: long crinkly or furry stuffed animals, stretchy fleece braids, small ropes just right for a little mouth, squeaky toys, bones, and chews of many types. Different pups like different things.

Often I see a floor littered with toys, though, and hear a despondent human report that the puppy "just doesn't care about toys and keeps going for our arms and legs." Hmm. When you were little, did you play all alone with your toys, or were they more fun with a friend? I promise that if you start to play with those toys like another puppy — get on the floor, toss something, chase after it, grab it, make a lot of happy noises — your pup will suddenly want that toy more than anything. Part of the reason a hand or leg is the preferred play item is that it guarantees human engagement.

Pup got your hand? Say "oops!" while you replace it with a rope toy and play tug. Chewing the chair leg? Give a quick "oops" and redirect to a bone. Repeat, over and over. In a few weeks, you will have a dog who seeks out those toys for mouthy play.

Why "oops" instead of "no"? Because, as training icon Pat Miller points out, it's hard to say "oops" in an angry tone. And why would we be angry with a puppy — one we kidnapped from Planet Dog — just for being a dog? Aim for the voice of a teacher, not a scary drill sergeant.

You'll need a dozen toys within your reach — but not within the puppy's reach. Toys are much more exciting if they aren't sitting out in the puppy's view all day every day. Keep a basket of them up high, and rotate through the toys to keep things interesting.

Don't forget, you have some potential toys that cost

nothing sitting around your house. Cardboard boxes, ice cubes, toilet paper rolls, and empty plastic water bottles (no cap!) can entertain puppy teeth for a good long time.

Feed Plenty and Often

What *exactly* should you feed? There's no one answer for all puppies, so I'll just note that diet affects everything. If you notice troubling physical or behavioral issues, remember to include diet among the possible causes and solutions.

The primary food mistake I see caring owners make in the first few months is this: They don't feed their puppy enough! The culprit is that darn chart on the back of the package, which fails to account for the fact that individual metabolisms and activity levels vary dramatically. That's why sometimes a very lean, jumpy, mouthy puppy shows up to my playgroup unable to play nicely or take turns with treats. The poor thing is hungry. At pickup time, I suggest to the owners that they feed 1.5 times as much per day for a week. (For example, if they're feeding two cups a day, now they'll feed three.) They're usually hesitant, but always come back a week later amazed that their pup was immediately way more pleasant to be around and sleeping much better. Lest the vets groan at this paragraph, I will emphasize that later in life it is easy to end up with an obese dog! My "feed more if they seem to need it" advice applies *only* while they are growing so very fast. Is your pup ravenous at every feeding? Trust your gut as you look at the pup in front of you, and take that quantity chart with a grain of salt.

Use Food to Build Great Behavior

Beyond "what" and "how much," you want to consider the surprisingly interesting question of "when" to feed your puppy. While the easiest protocol is to keep feeding puppies three times a day until they're past their super-fast-growing stages — typically at four to five months old — that's not the full answer. The smarter (and more challenging) approach is to use food all day as a teaching tool. After all, each morsel of kibble is an opportunity to create a positive impression. If you dump thirty pieces in a bowl to be gobbled in thirty seconds, you're throwing away gold. You'll have amazing results if you do one or more of the following instead:

- **Dump that kibble into a treat pouch** and use each piece to play "find it" on your morning walk to keep pup moving forward and not biting the leash: Just toss a piece right in front of pup's nose and say, "Find it." At first he may need you to point it out, but once he realizes those words always mean there's food on the ground, he'll get better and better at searching it out. Voilà! You have a pup eager to walk in the direction you want to go. As the weeks go by, you can use that treat pouch to reward the pup whenever he's at the sweet spot by your left knee; when he sticks with you as you change tempo, dramatically saying "fast-slow-fast-slow"; and when he checks in with eye contact. Soon you're going to love that those walks are filled with engagement, just because you decided to feed meals as you go instead of in a bowl!

- **Put kibble in a jar by the puppy apartment gate,** so that you're ready to teach and reward great greeting behavior when you enter, when the kids come home from school, or when guests come to see the pup. You can start with a food scatter from the other side of the gate (even a preschooler can toss a handful on the floor!) and progress to asking for sits and rewarding puppy with a piece of kibble. That creates a nice pattern of interaction that doesn't involve jumping and biting. Teaching pup to "touch" his nose to an outstretched hand is a great way to redirect a jumpy hello as you open that gate and enter the puppy apartment. Having kibble easily available for anybody to use to teach what we humans see as nice, polite engagement can quickly transform puppy chaos.

- **Use rubber food toys (like Toppls).** Make it a practice to stuff a few of these with a mash of kibble, plain yogurt, plain pumpkin, and maybe a little peanut butter, and put them in the freezer to make them last longer. You'll be so thrilled they're there when you want to create a positive association with the crate, entertain your pup when you have a Zoom meeting, or distract your pup when you have guests.

Food is a powerful training tool, communicating quickly and effectively across species. Sure, you could use "treats" in any of these situations, but by simply using your dog's nutritious, balanced food, you'll feel free to be generous instead of worrying you're treating too much. For sure, this method requires more effort than straight bowl-feeding — but then again, who knows how much effort it's saving by training your pup *not* to chew, destroy, jump up, or pull! The tricky thing is to keep track of how much you are feeding and to make sure it's roughly evenly distributed throughout the day. Maybe you measure the day's kibble into thirds, and breakfast goes in the morning walk pouch, lunch is a Toppl, and dinner is lots of fun training games with the kids.

One last word on the timing of food involves nighttime sleep. In the four hours before you put the puppy to bed for the night, don't feed more than a few morsels for training because you want that belly empty for sleeping. Same concept for water — just a few sips in that time frame.

Work Up to Leash Walks

Soon enough you'll be having fun adventures out in the world with this puppy, but don't expect to be able to pop on the leash and walk around the block on day one. Typically, an eight-week-old pup is just getting used to a collar and has never experienced a leash. Some adjust easily to the feeling, while others think the leash is a weird, scary trap, and they freak out when they feel that pressure. (Understandable, no?)

The key is to break down the experience into stages, and progress at the puppy's pace:

- Use a super-light leash, like those for a toy breed or a cat.
- Beginning inside where she's confident, attach the leash and let your puppy drag it around as you toss treats on the ground ("Find it!"). When she grabs the leash with her mouth, you can redirect by

distracting her ("Find it!") or starting a fun game of tug with her favorite toy.

- Pick up the end from time to time, moving around with her so that it does not tug on her neck. Don't pull her! We're helping her gradually get comfortable with the feeling of that slight weight.

- Continue having these short (a few minutes) leash play sessions inside until you can walk a few steps together as you toss treats on the floor. This process can take an afternoon or a week.

- From a puppy's perspective, the leash isn't the only intimidating part of this whole walk thing — resistance also comes from an unfamiliarity with the world outside. There's a lot to get used to: cars, bikes, strollers, steps, strangers, oh my! Your puppy may need a little time to adjust to all that. Let puppy watch things go by at a comfortable distance before expecting her to walk close to them. It helps to hang out regularly on your front stoop, doing nothing but observing, which is a highly underrated dog activity! You can add some tiny bites of something delicious like hot dog to create a positive association with anything potentially worrying: A loud truck noise is followed by a yummy treat. That order is important! We want the scaryish thing to predict something good, rather than yummy food predicting a scare.

Once your pup is ready to venture beyond the home, support her with a happy voice, a no-rush vibe, dance-y steps, and treats. Pulling your pup along will set your progress way back by interfering with that critical lesson #1 about trust. (If the person who's supposed to be your rock in a new situation were dragging you toward something that scared you, how would it change your feelings about whether you were safe with him?)

A wonderful secret weapon in the quest for forward movement can be a calm neighbor dog. Even the most reluctant pup will often suddenly jump into action given the chance to follow another dog.

Make the Crate a Happy Space

Crates can be a lifelong godsend — wonderful for both dogs and their owners. The key is taking the time to introduce them positively and using them in such a way that they feel like a relaxing, safe space to your pup. It's worth taking care with this, because having a dog who's happy in a crate enables stress-free entertaining, travel, vet stays, and so on. Here's how to get started on that path:

- Keep an open crate in the main area you've gated off to become the puppy apartment.
- Put the pup's favorite bed in there so that it's the obvious place to go to sleep. (Mind you, some pups prefer to sleep on cold flooring, and if that's your pup's habit, then remove the snuggly bedding!)
- Try covering the crate with a blanket to make it more like a nice dark den.
- Drop little pieces of kibble in there throughout the day so that pup develops the habit of checking inside to see if there's a treat.

- If pup goes in on his own, sneak over and drop in something delicious.
- If you're feeding regular meals in a bowl, do it in the crate. Close the door while he's eating, then immediately open it afterward. Now pup is connecting crate time with something reliably happy.
- Once pup is regularly going in on his own, experiment with giving a safe, long-lasting chew (like a frozen Toppl filled with a yummy and nutritious kibble–peanut butter–yogurt mash) and then closing the door. Again, as soon as pup is finished, open the crate to prevent any moments of panic.
- Once pup has some experience being inside the closed crate with food to enjoy, you can begin experimenting with closing the door for naps. Does your pup tend to zonk out after a big walk in the morning? Choose that time to put him in the closed crate with a Toppl. Ideally, he'll nod off after he finishes chewing. Be sure to be ready to open the door the moment he wakes up to avoid that feeling of panic.

After a week of using this gentle approach, the puppy tends to be happily settled into a routine of being crated for an hour or two several times a day.

Sure, Sleep with Your Puppy

The first night with a new puppy brings a dilemma: How can you supervise a peeing, chewing puppy if you're asleep? The most common solution is to contain the pup in a pen or crate. If you opt for that, the first week you'll want to be sleeping right next to it to offer comfort to your little one, who will be feeling lonely without littermates. You can put the crate or pen next to your bed, where you can reach your hand between those bars, or set it up next to the couch and sleep there temporarily. Still, there will likely be some crying.

If your gut tells you to start off with this puppy in bed with you...please go ahead and try it! Sleeping cuddled with a puppy works beautifully for many. Often the humans end up getting better sleep, because pups who are used to snoozing in a warm, breathing puppy pile adjust quickly to snuggling with you instead. It's possible to get a nice six-hour sleep that very first night with an eight-week-old, with zero crying (or peeing). Obviously, you need to be ready to sprint outside in the morning carrying that pup! You'll regret it if you decide to take your own potty break first...

If you don't want to sleep with a dog in your bed forever, you can transition the pup to a crate in a few days or weeks. By then the pup will have adjusted to her new family and will be accustomed to the crate thanks to her daytime naps. (But don't be surprised if you find that middle-of-the-night doggy snuggle in bed to be quite comforting for the humans!)

Socialize — at Puppy's Pace

All new puppy families face one urgent issue that's easy to miss: socialization. To feel comfortable in our wider world, our puppies need positive firsthand experience with a variety of people, animals, sights, sounds, and surfaces. It's wonderful to have an adult dog who can roll with new situations instead of being completely unsettled by, for example, kids bouncing a ball, men in hats, tile floors, garbage trucks, narrow stairs, or the sight of another dog! We have a golden opportunity up front, during early puppyhood, to move the needle toward lifetime confidence and fend off fear and skittishness. Socialization is easy to work on if you know how important it is in the beginning.

A robust body of research shows that puppies have a short window where they're particularly wide open to new experiences. After that, somewhere around four months of age, biology essentially tells puppies that if they haven't seen it before, it might be a threat. We want to counteract that by teaching our pups to feel comfortable with novelty itself. We could never expose pups to everything under the sun, but we *can* teach them that seeing something new generally turns out great.

Right from the beginning, try to make a point of exposing your pup — *in a gentle, positive way* — to new things. Warning: Plunking a new puppy on the sidewalk in the middle of a parade, or letting every stranger reach over and touch him, is the opposite of good socialization. When in doubt, think observation over immersion, and quality over quantity. Watch your pup's subtle body language and always adjust accordingly. Start at low-intensity experiences (farther away, quieter) and only increase intensity as pup shows he's relaxed.

You can easily start in your own home. Turn regular household activities like vacuuming and hair-drying into solid socialization opportunities by approaching them at your pup's pace. Make a point to do things like carrying a big box, moving a chair, playing unexpected music, and wearing something odd every day (a hat, a hoodie, a backpack), which will go far in terms of teaching your pup to roll with changes. Don't forget to pair these experiences with your own cheery demeanor, happy voice, and treats!

Before long, to make the most of this spongelike time, you have to head out into the world. Walk by a playground and let him observe kids who are running. Watch the puppy closely. Is he interested? Great, carry on. Nervous? Back up and let him watch from farther away. Allowing for that kind of low-risk data gathering is wonderful socialization! Many people make the mistake of thinking their puppy has to directly encounter things/people/dogs for it to "count." Nope!

Maybe a helicopter will go overhead or a car will honk — follow that with a small bite of cheddar cheese. Go to a friend's house when her wheelchair-using grandma is visiting so pup can learn that different spaces, odd-seeming equipment, and older humans just mean yummy treats!

You now have the perfect excuse to reconnect with your family, friends, and neighbors: "Help me teach my pup to love all humans!" Invite a few new folks over every week, even just for a few minutes, and let pup choose the level of interaction. Mind you, don't invite your squeal-and-grab friends — the whole point is for the pup to experience this as positive.

Find the Right Doggy Friends

A special subset of socialization is learning about other dogs. A puppy who is gently, carefully exposed to half a dozen very nice dogs up close — and many more at a comfortable "let's just pass by across the street" distance — is set up to be more comfortable around dogs for a lifetime. That makes all your dog walks, holidays, and vacations so much easier.

The safest way to do this is to rely on your network. Which of your responsible friends has a calm dog who's good with puppies? Go for an on-leash walk with them, and if things are going well, progress to some unleashed hangout time afterward. Then repeat, and expand by going through the same process with a handful of different dogs.

In addition to adult dogs with great temperaments, aim to find an appropriate puppy friend who belongs to a trustworthy neighbor. Puppies need to run, wrestle, and mouth things! Find yours a like-minded little buddy, and those classic needs can be met in twenty-minute playdates a few times a week. It's worth the effort to search hard for the right match. You'll be each other's saviors — and it'll turn the puppyhood phase into an absolute pleasure.

Mind you, puppy play requires good supervision and intervention at first so that the pups learn how to play without hurting or scaring each other. Sniffing through a gate and maybe going on a leashed walk together is a perfect beginning. Later, once pups are romping free together, you may need to interrupt frequently when play gets too rough. To do that, you can call everyone over to sit for treats, encourage them to play tug together by putting part of the rope in each pup's mouth, or start a group walk around the perimeter of the yard. Those activities tend to bring down arousal levels so pups can start up play again at an intensity that's more enjoyable. Play should feel balanced and reciprocal. If you aren't sure how things are going, try a "consent test": Pull the pups apart, and see if they *both* want to get back to playing together. If not, it's time to call it quits for the day and try again next week.

Of course, a local puppy class, which are often offered by humane societies or training centers, can provide an easy way to connect with other puppies. Some are fantastic, run by educated trainers who really know how to facilitate a positive experience for each pup. But others do more harm than good, offering "puppy play" that is poorly supervised. The best approach is to observe a class first, and if you opt in, just remember that you can step out if your pup is uncomfortable.

But What About Immunization?

The tricky part about all this socialization: Your pup won't be fully immunized against parvovirus and distemper until around four months of age. In the past, vets recommended keeping your pup home until two weeks after the last vaccination in the series. That isolation does keep pups safe from parvo and distemper, but it can be a sad recipe for behavioral disaster, since they miss out on their sensitive socialization period. Adult dogs who are afraid of new things are difficult to live with and can even be dangerous. As a result, many modern vets now offer more nuanced advice: Introduce your puppy to the world outside the home, but be smart about it. The best guidance is to keep away from unvaccinated dogs and the places they might hang out — but make a point of getting your puppy out and about in a careful manner. (For more on this, google the American Veterinary Society of Animal Behavior 2018 Position Statement on Puppy Socialization.)

Train for Connection

Sometimes people report with amazement that they just taught their ten-week-old puppy to sit in one session: "She is sooooo smart!" Of course, they're absolutely right.

In fact, we've found it's amazingly easy to teach our four-week-old foster puppies to sit and touch. By eight weeks they gleefully spin on cue, their exuberant recall (coming when called) is 100 percent, and we might even have a "down" in the mix.

Our point: Puppies *are* so smart indeed, and it is never too early to start training when you're using a positive, reward-based approach. Your puppy is a sponge and is learning something every minute anyway. You might as well be intentional about what you teach!

Of course, the topic of what to officially teach, and how, is beyond the scope of a chapter aiming to be a quick-start guide! You'll find comprehensive information on training in *Welcoming Your Puppy from Planet Dog*, but here's a starter pack of half a dozen things to work on the very first week with an eight-week-old puppy:

- **Name recognition.** Say the puppy's name, and the second she makes eye contact, give her a "yes!" and a treat.

- **Come.** Restrain yourself from the common habit of constantly calling your pup throughout the day — when she's having a grand time doing something else — which will essentially teach her to ignore the word *come*. Instead, arm yourself with a particularly yummy treat. Wait until your puppy is already heading your way and then enthusiastically start calling her. She'll come, and then you can reward her with a treat she'll really notice. Do that over, and over, and over. Next, start playing the recall game every night, where two or more of you (borrow a neighbor if you live alone!) call her back and forth and reward her with delicious treats. Why the special food? Because this is the cue that may save your dog's life. Let's say she escapes into the road. Since you've trained it in such a happy, head-turning fashion, when you call "Come!" muscle memory will make her spin on a dime and return to you.

- **Sit.** Lure the pup's first sit by holding a treat right in front of the nose and moving that hand up and back until you've guided pup's body into a sit. The second the bottom hits the floor, you exclaim "Yes!" and produce a treat. With progress, you change from a treat lure to a hand signal, and eventually the pup doesn't need a physical prompt at all — a simple verbal cue will do the trick.

- **Touch.** This cue may be the most underrated of all! Simply teach pup to touch her nose to a hand that's open and outstretched to the side. Even a preschooler can use this cue, which makes it a wonderful way to redirect jumping. Once it's established, if pup isn't coming when you call, say "Touch" and watch her run over to you. Need to get your now-150-pound Newfoundland off the couch but you haven't taught the "off" cue? Try standing back a few feet and asking for a touch.

- **Spin.** What's wonderful about teaching dogs to spin (circle around one time) is that it's impossible to feel stressed-out about teaching it. After all, it's just for fun, right? That relaxed attitude leads to a terrific training vibe, and pups tend to pick up that spin right away. The trick, as you're luring pup to move in a circle, is to keep the treat low, and to move it slowly at first — right in front of the nose. Once your pup knows "spin," it's a fun party trick that builds both canine and human confidence.

- **Find it!** It's always a funny moment when we trainers start teaching clients to toss food on the floor and say "Find it" to their pups. At first, they must want their money back! But soon enough, when their puppy reliably understands that those two words mean it's worth it to search the ground, the owners realize they have a magic solution to jumping and biting. A pup who's sniffing the floor has four paws on the ground and a muzzle directed there too. "Find it" is a great cue to use when people enter the house or approach on a walk. Once you're in the swing of it, you'll use this cue in so many different circumstances to entertain, distract, and redirect.

If you're thinking there's no rush, and you don't really care if your puppy does all those things yet, we get it. But this early teaching is about something much bigger than individual actions like "sit," "down," and "stay." It's about connection. When you introduce this fun game of training, a key light bulb goes on. Puppy learns she has agency here on Planet Human, earning something she wants by listening! That's the foundation of a lovely life for her, and for the two of you together.

Chapter Three

Managing a Senior and a Puppy, Together

We've given you a quick overview of both seniorhood and puppyhood. Now it's time to help you think through how to manage both ends of the age spectrum at the same time. Here are the questions to ponder, with suggestions for dealing with each issue.

When folks consider bringing a new puppy into their household with a senior dog, here's what they picture:

- The puppy will bring the old spark back to their senior!
- Their senior will sweetly take the pup under his wing, teaching and modeling.
- They'll nap contentedly together in the same dog bed, even though there's a second one right next to it.

We love all of that, and we truly hope it's in the cards for you.

But we've learned that our clients' daydreams typically fail to include the other potential side of the senior-and-puppy experience. Since surprises are the enemy of great dog ownership — we're not at our best when we're thrown for a loop — in this section we'll shine a light on the challenges that tend to arise. We don't mean to burst your bubble, but balancing the needs of opposite ends of the age spectrum can be tricky.

In fact, what kick-started the writing of this book is that we, like so many trainers and vets, see situations where the addition of a puppy was probably not the right call. Timing plays a big role, and often, bringing in the puppy a year earlier (when the senior was in better shape) or later (after the senior's passing) would have been better for everyone. In the worst cases, vulnerable senior dogs can end up no longer feeling comfortable in their own homes, forced to choose between fending off an energetic puppy or opting for isolation away from the humans they love. Puppies can wind up being resented because their humans, who are already stretched in caring for their declining senior, forgot how demanding puppyhood is. And humans can find themselves enjoying neither their beloved dog's twilight nor the puppy's precious first months.

Our point: This is a big decision. Adding a puppy might go just as beautifully as you hope, but it's not a slam dunk. Preparation (of both the home and the mindset) is your secret weapon. Here are some key questions you'll want to think through.

How Will You Introduce Your Puppy to Your Senior?

Often we trainers see folks a month after they've added a puppy. They contact us because they had assumed the pup and the senior would have "worked it out by now." But instead, the interactions have escalated from questionable to clearly worrisome. At that point, we have a harder task because a pattern has been established.

Remember this: First impressions matter! Take your time to carefully anticipate the introduction, and plan to manage the relationship quite a lot during those first few weeks. If you do that really well, you may find you're over the hump very quickly.

Here's What Works

- **Set up a gate or pen the day before** so the moment you walk in with the puppy, you'll have an easy way to keep the dogs separate. The day you bring the puppy home you're going to be so excited that you won't be thinking clearly in the moment. Often folks assume it'll be fine, operate on the fly, and later feel regret. That's so easy to avoid by simply mapping out the initial greeting ahead of time. Don't just walk in holding the pup and cradling her in front of your senior. Don't just put one or both on a leash. Instead, use that gate or pen you set up in advance. With that gentle barrier, the dogs can safely investigate each other without anyone getting overwhelmed or hurt. For an even better setup, design it so that each dog has a spot where they can retreat out of eyesight of the other.

The goal here is to give each dog a clear sense of agency. We don't want them feeling trapped in an uncomfortable situation. When you use a gate or pen, they're on their own four feet, and they can choose to move closer or farther away. They aren't confined in anybody's arms, and nothing is tugging at their necks. Another plus: The humans have their hands free in this setup, so they can more easily help in other ways.

- **Be patient.** Don't be in a rush to move the relationship along too quickly. The beauty of the pen/gate setup is that the dogs can advance their friendship safely. Sure, you're eager to see them romping together and sleeping snuggled up. But this is one of those situations where you need to go slow to go fast. Make sure each of those dogs feels comfortable and happy with the other before you give them a chance to interact without that barrier. (Have you ever seen how zoos introduce a new animal to those already in the exhibit? They set up a see-through barrier that allows safe acclimation at whatever pace is necessary.)

- **Observe body language.** Get in the habit right from the get-go of observing body language very closely. Are the dogs choosing each other or moving away? Are they loose and wiggly (good) or stiff and staring (not good)? You can even video-record interactions and watch them later, because you'll see things you missed in real time. The better you are at reading body language, the more effective you'll be at supporting their friendship.

- **Take the lead with controlled activities.** Activities where the dogs are together but not forced to interact are ideal for building a neutral-to-positive feeling. With no distractions, the dogs are super focused on each other and feel pressure to react in some way. You can make it much easier on them by offering some easy, positive distraction to lower the intensity. Keeping the dogs on opposite sides of the barrier, do a little easy training (for example, repetitions of "sit" or "touch" for a treat) together. Or try a meandering sniffari outside if you have an extra human to help. (Leashes are key for this, since the puppy may be obsessing over the senior or vice versa.)

- **Introduce a new treat.** Want to help your senior feel cheery about the new pup in those early days? Bring out an amazing new treat your older dog has never had before. (Feta cheese? Hot dogs? Dried fish?) Make a point of having that treat available only when the puppy is around.

How Will You Protect Your Senior from Puppy Energy?

Keep in mind that for a senior, "playing" with a puppy is entirely different from playing with a fellow adult dog. It's natural to assume that if your older dog has always played well with his buddies, he will love having a puppy to play with at home. But — unlike those solid adult dog friends — puppies have not yet fully developed their social skills. They constantly jump in faces, bite too hard, grab tender body parts, and pounce unexpectedly. They haven't yet learned that other dogs don't enjoy all that.

Perhaps you're thinking that your senior dog is just the one to teach the puppy canine manners and communication skills. Well, that can be true, to a point. But the best lessons are taught by a *willing* professor, not one acting under duress. Expecting your senior to babysit the rude toddler around the clock is unfair. (After all, the dogs didn't choose this living situation — the humans did.) If you want your senior to guide well, interacting with the puppy must be optional, or you'll find your puppy gets the wrong lessons. If you don't manage carefully, your puppy may learn from your senior that most canine interaction consists of growling and snapping. That does not bode well for their relationship or for the puppy's ability to have healthy dog friendships in the future.

Finally, add into the calculation the most important point of all: A typical senior has begun to decline physically. They have anywhere from minor aches to obvious tender spots that they protect. They may have begun to lose eyesight or hearing. (See chapter 1.) That means the incoming puppy missile is not just irritating but actually scary for them. (Mind you, even if you are a very caring owner, your senior may have diminishment that you are not aware of!)

A senior dog may feel vulnerable because of that natural physical decline, which can result in unwelcoming behavior you never would have anticipated: "Oh my gosh, I've never seen her snarl like that!" So if you bring a puppy into the household, your first priority is to protect your senior's peace — both physically and psychologically. If your older dog would rather relax into long naps but is perpetually on guard because an enthusiastic, full-of-energy pup might barrel in at any moment, you may be letting her down. Just because she's being "nice" about it — that is, hasn't growled, snapped, or bitten — doesn't mean it's okay! Often when I hear folks talk about how tolerant an old dog has been with a puppy, I think, "Please don't put that sweet old soul in a position where she constantly has to tolerate stuff." She's earned her peaceful, undisturbed days.

Now that we've thoroughly depressed you, keep in mind that in your particular situation, things might work great! Much will remain unknown until these two individuals are together under one roof.

Here's What Works

- **Set up separate spaces.** When you're not there to actively supervise, keep a puppy and an old dog separated. Yep, we know that's easier said than done, and it's not what you were picturing. But it is frankly *the* most important concrete piece of advice in this chapter. Maybe the puppy is in a pen or a crate, or there's a gate between the two dogs. It's possible this will only be necessary for the first weeks — or it may be a good idea forever. Your sharp observational skills will tell you which.

- **Observe.** When you're around to actively observe and manage, help make their interactions feel safe to them both. Watch and respect body language. Is each one choosing to interact with the other? Is either of them trying to move away?

- **Don't correct.** Do not try to manage their interactions by "correcting" either dog! Don't hover and say "no" or otherwise show how displeased you are. They most likely have no idea what in particular you're talking about — it's easy to misread that "no" — and all you're doing is adding more stress to an already confusing situation. The dogs may just think, "Wow, whenever the other dog is nearby, Mom's all tense and mad, so now I don't like the other dog."
- **Welcome the growl.** In particular, never discipline an older dog for growling, snarling, or snapping! Those are golden communication clues that we want to support. Those critical signals can do two things: (1) teach the puppy the senior's boundaries, and (2) alert the humans to fix the situation before anybody gets hurt. Growling or snapping that lasts for more than a few seconds is your sign to spring into action and adjust the scene.
- **Lead the activity.** If you can see that the puppy is being too much for your senior, initiate a more controlled activity — a joint walk or a fun, simple training session. Call them over to "sit" or "touch" for treats. Or you can experiment with tug or fetch — either just with the too-energetic pup or maybe with both dogs. All these options change the dynamic from a one-on-one free-for-all to something structured with your leadership.
- **Separate, cheerfully.** If the above-mentioned efforts fail to change the energy the puppy's bringing to the interaction, you'll need to separate them. Will you take the puppy up the street for a playdate

with a neighbor dog? Crate the puppy with a stuffed Toppl? Confine the senior behind a gate with a bully stick while you have a fun training session with the puppy outside? Be careful with your approach so that nobody feels punished just for the life stage they're in.

Are You Willing and Able to Tire Out Your Pup Elsewhere?

A bored puppy bursting with energy is the very last thing you want your senior dog to have to put up with. A puppy's first choice for fun is almost always another dog. No matter how delightful of a human you happen to be, your puppy is going to keep seeking out your other dog if he's in reach. Dealing with the adoration of a puppy 24-7 is an exhausting job for most dogs, but it's especially distressing for a senior dog.

The happiest senior-and-puppy matches are the ones where the puppy has plenty of outlets — other than the senior — for all that puppy energy. When they can meet their needs elsewhere, puppies return to their senior nicely spent. They say hi to their old dog sibling with a nice sniff and flop down to relax. Now *that's* a puppy an old dog can start to like! You might even finally see the senior actually approach the puppy: "Hey, um, I haven't seen you much today..."

Here's What Works

- **Puppy friend playdates.** New owners underestimate the life-altering effect of finding a BFF puppy of a similar age who lives up the street. Daily playdates like this have a miraculous impact on a puppy's household demeanor. Half an hour every morning with Max the Mix can make Luna the Lab suddenly seem almost civilized at home. It takes the edge off, because the puppy's natural bitey/wrestly needs have been met. The pup, now nicely balanced, is much more able to heed a message from Senior to chill out.

- **A realistic, stand-up stuffed dog!** It's natural for the puppy to want to bite or wrestle with the other dog who's on the scene, but that constant need is too big of a burden for a senior dog to carry. One remarkable solution for those first tough weeks is to bring in another "dog" who'll be willing to play every time: a realistic-looking, stand-up, life-size stuffed dog. Training industry leader Kim Brophey's Family Dog Mediation course details what she calls "the Karl Hack" (named after a stuffed dog she'd named Karl): You get your pup going with this fake friend during the witching hour when the pup truly needs something. I know you're thinking that can't be much different than the other stuffed toys the puppy ignores, but I promise, these more realistic-looking "friends" can be a lifesaver. Mind you, they won't last forever! This robust play may require a few repairs to keep the stuffing in, followed by an eventual retirement. That's okay, because I typically recommend Karls only for the first month or two, and only for maybe twenty minutes at a time, just to take the edge off.

- **Adult dog playdates.** Find an adult dog nearby who actually loves playing with puppies. The most likely candidates are just past puppyhood themselves, but there are also some fabulous older "nanny dogs" who remain reliably terrific with the little ones. Set them up for success with a great environment where they have room to romp a bit and ideally have hidey-holes in bushes, under benches, or behind sofas where either can retreat for a moment. The introduction, as always, needs to be careful and slow, ideally through a pen, gate, or fence where the two dogs can sniff and you can see good body language developing. Watch closely to make sure the play is going to be safe, and then thank your lucky stars you have this dog to make your puppy's world bigger and take some of the burden off your older dog.

- **Walks with friend dogs.** Find an adult dog nearby who, while perhaps not eager to romp and wrestle, is a great prospect for a mutual walk. Even just being around another dog can help scratch your puppy's deeply ingrained itch to be with his own kind. Having a daily walk around the block with a nice neighbor dog can truly render a pup less obsessive about an older sibling dog.

- **Fun human play.** Be as fun as a dog! Often folks tell me their puppy doesn't like any of the toys they bought. I come in and see a floor littered with toys and a puppy whining in the pen. Here's the thing: Nobody likes to play alone! You have to get in there and make those toys come to life. Pretend you're a fellow puppy. Grab that stuffed snake. Run around, drop it, let him get it, then play chase. Make a point of rolling around on the ground, running around, being goofy. It's all too easy to let our senior dogs do the work of play. Instead, we can do it too. Bonus: It will strengthen your relationship with your puppy.

- **Enrichment.** Incorporate all sorts of natural Planet Dog enrichment into your puppy's life: chewing, digging, sniffing. Maybe that means making every mealtime a foraging opportunity, so that instead of a twenty-second snarf, it's a twenty-minute kibble hunt in the grass or a half-hour chew/lick of a frozen Toppl. Maybe it's walks in a park on a long line (a fifteen- or twenty-foot leash) where pup can sniff to his heart's content.

Ideally, you'll create a routine for your puppy that includes every one of these things, which will dramatically lighten the entertainment load your senior dog will otherwise carry.

How Much Flexibility Do You Have for Setup?

Creating a special, smaller home base — a puppy apartment — within the household is always key in puppyhood (see page 35). If your senior dog is basically in good shape and can still navigate the house well, then simply setting up a puppy apartment will do the critical work of ensuring your senior has an easy escape from puppy antics.

But what if your senior is at the stage where she *also*

needs a special, limited space because of incontinence issues, mobility issues that make the main house a danger, or cognitive decline that leaves her confused? Do you have a second space available to section off for her (see page 12)?

Here's What Works

- **Main-area puppy apartment.** The space you choose for your puppy needs to be in a main living area because they have so much to learn from humans! To develop well, they need to be interacting with their people, observing activity.

- **More secluded senior space.** When you have a puppy, your senior may prefer to spend a lot of time relaxing in an area of the house that's quieter. If she naps a lot, turning an office or a bedroom into her spot could be perfect.

- **Great gates.** If your senior still wants to be in the middle of the action, you can use gates and pens to section the main living areas into spaces for each dog. Gates and pens come in so many configurations, styles, colors, and materials these days that you can probably find something you won't completely hate. Don't despair until you've googled!

  How will it feel having those gates and pens to walk through and step over all the time? Speaking from experience, we think you'll just get used to it like we have. It's all temporary anyway, as needs change from one phase to the next. And frankly, those defined spaces make these stages of dog life so much easier and relieve so much stress that we easily get over the minor inconvenience and the fact that our house isn't exactly ready for a glamorous photo shoot.

Poop and Pee: How Much Patience Do You Have?

Everybody knows that potty training is going to be a major part of puppyhood, and they steel themselves for that process. What's often not on a dog owner's radar is that accidents on the floor can become an issue again a dozen years later. When you have an aging dog, incontinence often comes with the territory. Sometimes seniors feel fairly good physically and live happy lives but simply can no longer "hold it." (For more on senior incontinence, see page 15.)

That's never easy, but when you also have a puppy you're trying to potty train, it can become a disaster! The scent of urine will encourage a puppy to pee, which is why it's so important to clean up immediately using something that neutralizes odors (Nature's Miracle works well) when your pup has had an accident. But what if your older dog is filling the house with the scent of pee? That is a direct message to your puppy that inside is a perfectly appropriate spot to relieve himself. Uh-oh.

Here's What Helps

- **Pee pads in the senior's area.** Create a special area for your older dog (see page 12) and use pee pads there. While the puppy will probably still smell pee odor drifting from those pads, it's better than the puppy smelling pee on the floor throughout the house.

- **Diapers for the senior.** The best option might be to use doggy diapers on the senior. That way, any elimination (and its associated scent) is contained and less likely to impede the puppy's learning. Still, this is not ideal for your older dog, who may be thrown by the feeling of a diaper (see page 16).

Our fondest hope for you is that you have timing on your side here and your little puppy becomes fully potty trained before your senior experiences incontinence. In that case, you will have a better shot of your pup not responding to the scent of urine inside. If not, we're back to the lead question in this section: How much patience do you have? This is a tough one.

Will Your Whole Household Commit to Feeding Dogs Separately?

Whenever you add a second dog to a home, it's smart — and kind — to feed the dogs separately. So many clients come to us with the issue of one dog getting into the other's food, one dog growling at the other near a bowl, or the two dogs actually having a fight around the food.

We love "problems" like this! Just feed them separately. Done. There is no rule that good dogs must be able to eat close together. Perfectly wonderful dogs can live their whole lives being BFFs and be uncomfortable eating next to each other. So why would we add stress to their lives when there's no need for it?

Puppies in particular will toddle over to any old bowl and ignore signals from an older dog to back off. In our experience, that's the most common way a pup ends up with her first bite from a big dog. It ends up being pretty traumatic all around, which is such a shame because it's utterly unnecessary.

Even if no altercation ever happens, big, negative feelings can simmer internally. Why does that matter? If twice a day, every day, the dogs feel in competition for an important resource — "Dang it, she's so close. Is she going to get my stuff this time? I hate that." — that will interfere with the easy friendship we're hoping develops between them. How about instead setting them up to feel "Yay, here's my food" without any negative emotions regarding their sibling dog? There are plenty of ways to feed separately, and one of them will feel easy enough for you to incorporate into your routine.

Here's What Works

- Feed one dog in a crate and the other out of sight.
- Feed them on opposite sides of a gate, with one around the corner out of sight.
- Feed one dog in the bathroom.
- Feed one dog on the porch or outside.
- Feed them both in the kitchen but at opposite ends, with you standing in between the entire time, clearly (but cheerfully) using your body language to communicate they stay with their own bowls.

At some point it may seem that it is utterly fine to feed your particular dogs together. Maybe their relationship is terrific, they always want to be together, and they easily share toys and spaces and humans. As long as you're aware of the subtle signs to watch out for — eating super fast to finish before the other guy, side glances to see what the other one's up to — you may be ready to experiment with relaxing this approach.

Mind you, the same "separate for safety" rule goes for any kind of special treat that isn't swallowed immediately — bones, stuffed food toys, and so on. Set your canine friends up to stay friends by keeping them mercifully apart to enjoy those things. You will know by the way the dogs act if there's something you need to manage carefully. Maybe nobody cares about the Kong, but they're wild about the bully stick. Maybe nobody cares about the red ball, but the blue ball incites growling. We don't have to understand it, but we do have to observe it and help them stay out of trouble with each other.

The title of this section may sound dramatic, asking if your entire household will commit to feeding separately. But take it from us, very bad things can happen in seconds when one human who didn't believe this could be an issue puts an exciting resource on the floor. Please, have this discussion with everybody in the house.

What Will Your Dog Walks Be Like?

If you're used to getting your brisk ten thousand steps a day through dog walks, that will change once you add a puppy to the mix. Or perhaps it has already started to change as your older dog has slowed down.

Ideally for his development, a puppy's first few months

of walks are going to be meandering adventures full of stops and sniffing and observing. That's how he'll learn to feel confident in the world! You'll bring a treat pouch and encourage lots of engagement with you by rewarding eye contact. You'll play "find it," tossing kibble a few steps ahead to keep the pup walking generally forward with neither of you pulling. You'll ask for some sits and touches. It'll be a lovely bonding and happily exhausting experience — for your pup! But from the human point of view, that pace is very slow, so a dog walk in this phase doesn't really count in the exercise column. Why is that important? Because you'll realize that this half hour used to be a multitasking effort and now it's singly focused on the puppy.

More challenging news: These early puppy walks will likely not work well for your senior dog. Until you've made progress teaching a nice leash-walking pattern, the puppy will likely be all over your senior dog during a joint walk: jumping on him, biting his leash, and tugging. Your senior will want to escape the puppy. The leashes will tangle. You'll get really frustrated and come home and exclaim, "This is impossible!" You'll be correct. In the beginning it works much better to walk the dogs separately or to enlist a partner so each dog has a human and the senior can have space.

Where are you going to find the time for two separate walks, neither of which actually counts as exercise for you, since your senior has slowed down too? Well, if you're like us, you'll just drop some boring chores like making beds or paying bills! Kidding aside, the best way through this is to anticipate a different kind of dog walk for this phase.

Here's What Works

- **Relax expectations.** Keep your idea of what a walk "should" look like flexible. Things will change rapidly as a puppy matures. What's not possible in the first month might be doable in the second and easy in the third.
- **Use two humans.** In the very first few walks, it's smart to have both dogs and two humans. That way, the puppy will gain confidence being able to follow his sibling dog — but the extra human can keep that from becoming a tangled nightmare.
- **Two short (good) walks beat one (bad) long one.** Once pup is confident heading out on leash, separate walks are best for a while. Two very short walks (one for each dog) are better than one really frustrating longer one! If you are free to focus on the puppy, you can reward and therefore build better behavior. That brings you closer to the day when you *can* walk them together.
- **A sniffari works for everyone.** Going slowly and encouraging dogs to take in the scents all around them is a rewarding activity at both ends of the age spectrum. While it's hard to move forward at a brisk pace with a puppy and a senior, sometimes it works well to meander slowly through a park, sniffing particularly where the grass meets the woodland area. When the pace is this slow but the interest on the ground is high, the leashes tend to get tangled less.
- **Have a watch party.** Hanging out and observing on leash is also a terrific activity for both puppies

and seniors. Take the dogs to a park, set up a picnic blanket, and watch for interesting things. Bring your treat pouch so you're prepared to do a little bit of redirecting if necessary. Ideally, the puppy will be fascinated by seeing people/dogs/trucks go by at a distance and the senior will be content to chill out. (Remember, your puppy doesn't need a fast-paced walk to feel tired out! Just absorbing new information from the environment can be exhausting.)

Can You Make Time for Puppy Adventures — Without Depriving Your Senior?

One of your most important jobs in the first months with a new puppy is to make a point to carefully introduce her to the world. While there's a lot you can do at home to teach your pup to roll with new things, great socialization can really only happen out and about in the larger environment.

That doesn't mean taking your pup wherever you go! The only outings that work well are those you can dial up or down in intensity to meet your pup exactly where she is. For example, let's say you want to get your pup to feel comfortable around kids. An ideal scenario would be approaching a fenced playground where kids are having fun. (The fence is key because it gives you control over the distance, keeping the kids from swarming an unsure puppy.) If pup is interested and moving toward the sounds, great! If not, though, you'll want to stop a nice distance away and allow her to observe. Maybe that's plenty for today, and you come back the next day to see if the pup feels confident about getting closer.

That minute-by-minute adjustment factor is why good socialization takes time and attention. You can't be multitasking. You need to focus solely on the puppy's body language and be able to respond accordingly. If you have your senior dog (or your kids) with you, you can't do that, which means your effort at positive socialization may well backfire and teach all the wrong lessons.

Do you have time to do it right? Can you do maybe three twenty-minute adventures a week where it's just you and your puppy? Let's say you try the park, a friend's house, and Lowe's (which has a national policy to allow dogs). If you're squeezed for time in general, will this puppy adventure mean you'll be skipping some engagement with your senior (a little walk, a routine cuddle session), or will your senior be happy to nap?

Here's What Works

- **Plan ahead.** It is all too easy to intend to head out with the pup but then to see your older dog's sad eyes and decide just to stay home so nobody's left out. Don't do that! You'll pay the price later when your pup is skittish and uneasy out in the world. Instead, make a concrete plan for exactly when you'll take the pup out and about — and have an equally concrete plan for your senior at that time. Will she get a special frozen Toppl? Will she get to hang with the kids while they do their homework? Will your partner be cuddling with her on the couch? With a plan in place, you won't guilt yourself into skipping puppy socialization adventures.

What About When Your Senior Declines?

It's natural to wish for new beginnings and some fresh joy when you sense that losing your senior is around the corner. A puppy can be just the thing, truly! While the demands of puppyhood are high, so much fun and sweetness are folded into that package.

However, sometimes the timing turns out not to be on your side. Say you're *just* able to manage caring for both dogs and it feels like you're meeting everybody's needs. But then...your senior hits some bumps on the health road or truly begins to decline. That takes a lot of emotional energy. How will you feel as you're navigating meds and diagnoses and how to best support your old friend — when at the same time you're trying to find the time and energy to potty train and socialize a puppy?

Here's What Works

- **Build your village.** Instead of letting yourself be taken off guard by health challenges, anticipate them. Think through what kind of support you might need. Do you have loved ones who can step in and help fill in the puppy gaps while you focus on your senior — or vice versa? Can you create a daily dog care schedule for your family to make sure everything's covered? (And even include cuddling your senior. You don't want to think, a week after your senior's passing, that you were distracted and you ignored him at the end. Those thoughts are awful to deal with, so cover yourself by factoring this in.) Do you have a neighbor who wouldn't mind checking on the puppy when you're at the vet with your senior? Do you have a friend who'll keep your anxious senior company while you take the pup out for an adventure?

- **Prepare to grieve.** It's incredibly difficult to lose a dear old dog. Most of us end up wanting to crawl under the covers and just stay there. What if you have a puppy when that happens? And what if that puppy who was so cute last week now just strikes you as...a very poor substitute? Maybe you'd rather not even be around the puppy this week. This is so common! Don't worry — it turns around! But in the meantime, it's a good idea to (1) have that village ready to step in for the pup for a little while and (2) seek out whatever helps you: friends, a therapist, making a photo album or a slideshow, doing yoga, drinking tea and journaling about your memories of your senior's life (you'll find more on this in chapter 5, "Savoring the Sunset"). Soon enough you'll emerge. As they say, grief is just love with nowhere to go — but at some point, you'll be ready to pour that love back into your puppy.

What If It Turns into the Dream?

While we're trying to prepare you for the challenges that sometimes surprise people, it is absolutely possible that in fact you'll end up with that dream you were picturing in the beginning: The puppy did indeed reinvigorate your sweet old friend, and when they weren't playing, they were cuddled up together. The puppy was super easy to integrate into the family because she was shaped by your bestest boy.

There is just one more thing you'll need to give this beautiful scene a happy ending: You'll want to help your puppy to be okay when this period comes to an end and your senior passes on. If your puppy only knows life next to her big brother 24-7, she'll be in for a shock one day. Be sure to make time to take her on her own adventures, car rides, walks, and vet visits. Playing and building relationships with other well-socialized dogs will set her up with friends to continue enjoying when he passes. Also, work it into your routine that sometimes she stays home alone while her big brother goes out. We want to support her independence, so that she is fully ready to carry on with your family after having absorbed so many important lessons from your beloved senior. She will likely still grieve his loss, as will you, but in taking these preemptive measures, you will help her feel more secure when she becomes an only pup.

Chapter Four

Adding an Adult Dog Instead of a Puppy

Sometimes, once you really think about it, the extra commitment involved in puppyhood is simply too much to take on. But that doesn't mean bringing in another dog at this point in your senior's life is off the table. The right move for your household might be finding a well-adjusted adult who'll be able to join in without the extra challenges of potty training, chewing, socializing, and such.

While many of us are googly-eyed over puppies, a subset of humans believes the dream is finding the perfect adult dog to bring into the family.

They're not wrong!

If you pick the right one (more on that later), an adult dog:

- is potty trained
- no longer chews shoes and furniture

- no longer jumps up and mouths everyone
- can be safely allowed to roam unrestricted throughout the house
- can be left alone for hours at a time

While skipping these challenges is the most obvious benefit to choosing a dog past the puppy stage, there are plenty of other perks as well.

What You See Is What You Get

One of the very best things about adopting a dog who's past adolescence is that what you see is what you get. You don't have to wonder how big they'll get, what their coat will be like, or whether their ears will go up or down. You'll have a good sense of whether this dog, for example:

- enjoys other dogs
- likes to chase or wrestle
- snuggles in for TV time
- will be able to go with the flow around kids and strangers

You'll also have a realistic idea of what this dog's energy level and exercise requirements will be.

All those things can play a role in how easily and happily a new dog fits into your family. With an adult, you're much more able to set yourself up for the smoothest ride possible — and that can be a giant bonus when you've got an aging senior who requires more TLC than he used to.

The Puppy Socializing Is Already Done

Many folks feel it's "safer" to get a puppy because they don't want any behavioral surprises from a dog who may not have had an ideal background. The trouble with that thinking is that those people are assuming (1) the desired results are guaranteed when you do things right, and (2) it's pretty easy to do things right.

In reality, it can be challenging to get yourself up to speed enough to socialize a little puppy perfectly. And even if you do have the knowledge, the interest, and the bandwidth, sometimes you still end up with a dog who's not comfortable with something — maybe kids, or strangers, or other dogs, or being alone.

I've known people who chose not to adopt a wonderful two-year-old rescue — perfect for their situation — because they worried she'd have some hidden issue because of her unknown background. Then they got a purebred puppy. Two years later they "had to give her up" because she was biting people. The truth is that they didn't have the time to socialize well, which is the case for so very many people! Sometimes, you're better off adopting a dog who has learned about the world elsewhere.

Our point: You can size up an adult! What you see is what you get.

Easier Interaction with Your Senior

When you have a senior and you want to be sure interactions with a new dog go as well as possible, it might feel easier to start with what seems to be a tiny, less threatening option: a puppy. But often, the biggest terrors come in the youngest packages!

The right adult dog, in contrast, will already have solid doggy communication skills on board, and therefore may be less exhausting for your senior to deal with. For example, an adult will likely respond to the subtle signals your senior is giving when it's not the right time for play. In addition, adults play in a different way than puppies: Instead of constant mouthing and pouncing, there's more simple sniffing, with the occasional chase or wrestle. It's not unusual for a dog to hate hanging out with puppies but love playing with adults.

Less Work for You

There's no getting around the fact that doing puppyhood right means diving in and devoting a ton of time to this new little being. We need to teach an enormous amount to our puppies about life here on Planet Human. For many of us, that's time beautifully spent. It's a fun (not to mention adorable) journey with lots of wonder and bonding. And yes, it gives us the chance to shape this dog.

But that's not how puppyhood feels to everyone. Managing a new puppy can be exhausting. The idea that you have so much to teach may feel like a stressful to-do rather than a rewarding life phase. If you think you might be on that end of the spectrum and you might wind up wanting to speed through puppyhood and be finished with it (totally reasonable!), one way to do that is to skip it altogether and get an adult dog.

What Would Be the Best Match for Your Senior?

Adopting an adult means you can search for a dog who has already developed into the kind of dog you want, so let's figure out what that means for you. You can't find it if you don't know what you're looking for.

First, think about the impact on your senior dog. Ideally, this new dog will end up being a lovely friend and companion to your senior. At worst, we'd want the dog to simply be a neutral change for your senior.

- What kind of dog (size, gender, play style, energy level) does your senior typically like?
- What type of dog or dog behavior makes your senior uncomfortable?
- Is your senior way into attention? If so, think twice about getting a dog who is also going to demand a lot of attention. Your senior may hate that, and you'll feel guilty.

Is the Best Match for Your Senior Also the Best Match for You?

Once you've pondered what might be the best, kindest match for your senior, you might realize this does not line up with your own vision of the ideal next dog. Maybe you envision your next dog being one who is both super snuggly and very bouncy/energetic — but both of those things would be rough for your senior to put up with.

What are your other deal-breakers? Does your dog need to be relaxed around kids? Not very barky? Okay in a city environment? Unfazed by chickens? Maybe you can handle sandwich stealing and overexuberant greetings, but not resource guarding.

There's no clearly right answer here. Just a caution to think it all through. If you discover a dog who totally works for the humans, the senior dog, and the new dog…awesome. Otherwise, it could be that the happiest course of action is to fully enjoy your senior's sunset time without the complication of introducing a new dog.

Where Will You Find This Dog?

Thanks to our frenemy Google, it's easy to search for a dog. Alas, it's also easy to be led astray by incomplete information. So while it's perfect to start online, landing your terrific next dog is going to take some in-person work. Whether you go through a breeder, a rescue group, a shelter, or simply another owner who's giving up their dog, you'll want to gather as much information as you can, and then have a meet-and-greet — or two.

An adult dog is going to have a history. While it's nice to know that history, the most important thing to know is what the dog is like *now*. That's because sometimes a history sounds sad and terrible, but the dog who emerges from it is *amazing*. Sometimes a history looks great on paper, but that dog has a challenging issue or two that would make him a terrible match for you.

If you're interested in a dog who's being given up by his owner or one who's been in a foster home for a few weeks, you'll have a wonderful chance to ask a human who's lived with him great questions about what he's like. Ideally, you can go meet him in that environment, where he's comfortable, and get a sense of things. Get the humans talking, and listen closely! They know things you cannot from a one-hour visit.

If you're adopting a dog from a shelter, you have less to go on. That doesn't mean it's a bad choice! But be aware that a shelter environment is simply a lot different from a home environment. There will be things — both good and bad — that only show up once a dog starts to decompress and become more comfortable in a home. Sometimes the staff has a real sense of a dog and can tell you a lot. But sometimes the dog just came in and the only information available is a brief secondhand summary from a previous shelter. If the dog seems wonderful, he really might be! And if you're lucky, the shelter may let you foster-to-adopt so that you can take him home for a few days or weeks to see how it goes.

Another option is to enlist a (good, force-free, kind) trainer to help you either all the way through this search or right at the end as you're ready to say yes. A knowledgeable trainer may be able to provide some great perspective on what you're looking for and notice subtle body language (either promising or worrisome) that you might miss. (For example, a dog may appear wonderfully calm to a potential adopter, but a trainer might immediately see that he's actually shut down from the trauma, and so his true personality is not coming through.)

Pick Well, Then Introduce Carefully

The more you know about the adult dog you adopt, the more sure you can be that any surprises will be minor, such as finding out she's a little scared to go on a walk in the dark or she gets mouthy when she's overtired. Still, there will usually be some bumps in the road as you integrate a new dog into your family. If you've done your homework well, your next job is to take a deep breath and commit!

While it should indeed prove easier to adopt an adult than to live through a year of puppyhood, the path will be much happier if you still expect an intense first three weeks! Approach this introduction much as we suggest for the puppy introduction:

- Make use of safety barriers (pens, gates, leashes, tethers) at first. (Do pick a dog who does not have an existing issue with gates or leashes because those are key tools here.)
- Supervise at all times, or keep the dogs separate.
- Build positive feelings by keeping the senior's favorite things in place.
- Further build positive feelings by training with special treats when the dogs are together.
- If appropriate for both, try on-leash meandering sniffari walks together.
- Watch out for resource guarding! It's absolutely natural for dogs to guard things they view as important (food, bones, toys, beds, or people), and the newer they are to each other, the more likely it is that one of them will try to protect their resources by growling, snapping, or even biting. Set the dogs up for success by not leaving stuff they view as valuable lying around where it could cause a fight.

With this kind of careful start, you may find that your new adult dog is fully integrated into your family within a month! That's typically a much faster path to calm normalcy than puppyhood, and it may allow you to sustain your focus on your senior, which may feel very good to your heart indeed.

Chapter Five

Savoring the Sunset

Bringing a dog into the family opens us up to so much joy — and also to the pain of the inevitable goodbye. The stubborn fact is that a human's lifespan is about eight times as long as a dog's. From the very beginning we know the poignant truth: We'll likely outlive this loyal friend. As hard as that is, there is something beautiful about it too. We have the enormous honor and responsibility of walking next to this extraordinary creature from their beginning to end.

As you near your senior's last chapter, you can choose to "savor the sunset." Rather than being blind to what's happening and trying to force activities that don't work anymore — the hike, the playdate, the game of fetch — you can breathe in the simple perfection of this deep companionship. You can relish the chance to sit together in the sun and relax on the porch. And then, finally, when the moment comes, you can be ready to give your devoted friend the most pain-free passage possible.

We know — you're reluctant to even read this part of the book. Whether we're losing our dogs or our friends or our parents, we tend to turn away, trying to avoid the inescapable finality of death.

But there's good reason to force yourself to think through this tough topic in advance: The more you know what to expect, the more smoothly it will unfold for you and for your dog. You'll be better able to do justice to this beautiful animal and the bond you two have created together.

Dealing with Anticipatory Grief

While some owners have trouble facing the truth about their dog's advanced stage in life, others are so focused on a looming goodbye that it's hard for them to enjoy the moment. "Anticipatory grief" can start even before a dog is slowing down, and it can rob folks of the ability to be happily present in the time they still have.

In order to savor the sunset, you may need to train your mind to focus on "being here now." It's easier said than done, but one way to do this is to create memorable routines and experiences, for example:

- Start going to the coffee shop every Wednesday morning for a pup cup (the whipped cream treat so many shops now offer).
- Wind down every Sunday evening with a visit to the creek.
- Gift yourself with half an hour every morning on the porch — a coffee for you and a rubber LickiMat spread with pumpkin and yogurt for your senior.
- Be intentional about having TV cuddle time together every night.

- Make a bucket list of things you want to do with your senior, and take photos as you check off those events. (Mind you, make sure these activities are senior-appropriate, like arranging a visit from the neighbor who puppy-sat long ago. We don't want the bucket list to leave our old friend sore and achy!)

This kind of approach counteracts the feeling that time is slipping away and helps cut down on regret by giving you concrete proof of good times. Later on, having a slideshow on your phone filled with highlights from years of happy times will ease your heart.

Savoring the Sunset with a Puppy at Your Senior's Side

Having a puppy already settled in the family during a senior's end-of-life process can be tremendously helpful. A healthy, vibrant, and sometimes mischievous bundle of energy can be very soothing for our worried hearts. While puppies carry their own challenges — *don't eat this, don't chew on that, please stop humping* — those worries aren't sad, like the concerns of caring for a dog who is having difficulty with mobility.

Not only does the puppy bring a great sense of joy into your home, but overlapping the pup with your senior sometimes allows you to more quickly gain a deeper connection with your new dog. After your senior dog passes, it's comforting to sit with the fact that the new puppy knew your old friend. It feels like they've absorbed, from the best, how to be your trusted companion.

Practically speaking, it can be lovely to loop your puppy

into the ways you are making a point of "savoring the sunset" with your senior. A daily pattern of relaxing time on the porch or couch with your senior can end up teaching a wonderful "settling" behavior for the puppy. (Just make sure to start with the puppy confined with a chew, to make sure he doesn't ruin this time for your senior!) Some of your senior dog bucket list adventures can be your new puppy's "firsts," such as sharing an ice cream at the beach or taking a trip to the riverbank in the woods.

Another way to savor the sunset together is by doing a memorial photo shoot with both dogs. Or you could have the kids in the family write a little story or draw a picture with the two together. After your old dog has passed, these memories, photos, and visuals will help you appreciate that the new puppy was present during this precious time, even if it was chaotic.

Creating a Philosophy on Medical Intervention

Approaching the final phase doesn't look the same for every dog, but every owner will face decisions about medical intervention. A senior dog's decline can be a gradual, yearslong road that's mainly about, say, arthritis. Or it can be faster, such as with a metabolic disease like kidney failure. Or it might be shockingly steep, with an undetected cancer that suddenly creates a crisis.

The possible medical treatments available to you may run the gamut from a special diet to major surgery. The slower your dog's decline, the more time you'll have to feel out how you want to approach various types of intervention. Some decisions may feel easy, like adding a pain reliever for hard days or switching over to the special kidney-support food. But it gets complicated when the options presented are more invasive, have side effects, involve a tough recovery time, require stressful trips to the vet, or have a giant price tag.

It's one thing to weigh all that for a young dog who may have years ahead once you get the current crisis under control and who has youth and strength on his side as he rebounds. With seniors, the calculus changes. Which decisions will help our dear old friends have the highest quality of life for as long as possible? Which would, in fact, increase suffering?

While you can't know exactly what situations you'll face, it is incredibly helpful to have some general family discussions *before* anything serious is on the table. It is all too common for folks to have a senior dog who enters a medical crisis they didn't expect. They suddenly find themselves at a vet — maybe even an emergency clinic where they've never been before. A ton of new information comes at them quickly, and they need to make hugely influential decisions very fast. It is hard enough to lose a pet under the best of circumstances, but it's absolutely devastating to lose one after a shocking twelve-hour crisis involving a $5,000 Hail Mary treatment attempt that only puts the dog through phenomenal stress.

As hard as it is to do, you'll benefit from talking through possible scenarios at home — with your dog sleeping happily at your feet — before you ever get to this moment. You'll be able to think more clearly and weigh all the variables more logically when you don't have a dog in pain who requires your immediate decision-making. People who have never had to euthanize a pet before tend to begin these conversations thinking they'd "do everything" to save them, but once pressed with scenarios where medical intervention might just prolong suffering, they realize they have a more complex view. That's a really important idea to digest ahead of time! It's very difficult when that realization only kicks in a few days into a painful treatment with very low odds of success. Though it may feel distasteful, force yourself to include finances in this discussion. It is not unusual these days to face a $10,000 vet bill, and it can go even higher. Do you have insurance? If not, how much vet care can you afford? What will you do if your dog needs more than you can give? These are difficult issues, and hard to cover in the abstract, but it proves very helpful if you have at least broached the issue before you have actual decisions to make.

A special note here about college kids: Please loop them into this discussion before they head off. It is incredibly common for a family to face a crisis compounded by the absence of the one who was the dog's "person" for years and years. Even though it's difficult, have a heart-to-heart in person before there's an emergency.

The Balancing Act Around Suffering

A senior with a chronic medical condition that causes everyday pain or discomfort is suffering, so of course you'll want to offer relief. Sometimes you can try a pain medication and a change in environment — like pairing an anti-inflammatory med with blocking off stairs and adding more rugs — and begin to see your old friend perking up. Great!

However, as time goes on, the decision-making becomes more complex, and a balancing act begins. What if the intervention creates a different kind of suffering? Maybe a pain medication causes bad stomach issues, or a steroid results in insatiable thirst and a personality shift. Perhaps a supposedly simple lump removal heals excruciatingly slowly, requiring stressful follow-up visits for a dog who's terrified at the vet. That may be the time to start asking quite honestly:

- What is the goal?
- Are we fighting for more time?
- If so, is that extra time for our dog or for us? (All time is not equal in this calculation. Is a week that's filled with suffering the type of time that is worth fighting for? Where is that line?)
- Is one intervention leading to another and another?
- Is the fact that we don't want to lose our dog leading to interventions that increase her suffering instead of relieve it?

These can be muddy waters indeed. Often, it's not possible to know how your dog will respond to a treatment. Is that tricky surgery to remove the little lump going to result in a nightmare of complications? Or will your dog surprise everyone and sail through the anesthesia, have a quick and simple recovery, and be back to herself in three weeks? It is impossible to know for sure.

But eventually — as you track function, purpose, and joy and have honest conversations with your vet — you'll reach a point when you realize the kindest, most loving and respectful approach is to stop trying new things.

That, then, brings up the next big question: Do you wait for a natural death, or do you opt for euthanasia?

A "Natural Death" Sounds Better Than It Is

If you haven't lost a pet yet, you might have a vague sense that your dog will just get old and gray and slow, and then one day fall asleep on his bed and not wake up. If only it actually worked like that! The term *natural death* sounds so peaceful, doesn't it? Unfortunately, that soothing fantasy is something that keeps dog owners from preparing themselves to make better decisions as their dog declines.

While a small percentage of dogs really are basically feeling okay and living full lives until they simply don't wake up one day, that's the exception. What's far more common for those who experience a natural death is to go through periods (days, weeks, or months) of incredibly stressful suffering. They may have increasing anxiety because of their decreasing function. They may endure severe pain and labored breathing.

Dogs are much more inclined than humans to hide their frailty (it's a survival mechanism), which is why sometimes owners are not at all aware of just how much their dog is already suffering. That may be why death sometimes seems sudden to owners. (But *you* won't miss the decline because you learned in chapter 1 to track the key things — function, purpose, joy. See page 24. You're going to notice subtle signs that point to suffering.)

Once a dog's final decline becomes unmistakable, it is very difficult to witness. Sometimes the natural death that people knew full well was approaching somehow winds up seeming sudden and urgent and stressful because their dog is gasping and crying. Rather than the peaceful sleep they had anticipated, the last memory of their dog is filled with anguish and suffering all around.

Planned Euthanasia Offers Peace

People who have experienced the death of a pet before almost always opt for a scheduled, safe, legal, professionally administered euthanasia the next time. While it is absolutely never an easy decision to make, opting for euthanasia is often the best choice:

- It minimizes your dog's suffering, whether by hours, days, weeks, or months.
- It shortens the time you and your family are suffering as you watch your loved one in pain.
- It gives you control over the end. You can plan when and where your friend will breathe her last breath. You can make sure the important humans are at her side.
- It helps you to be as emotionally ready as possible, so you can give your dog the best of yourself at the end.
- It typically gives you a peaceful last memory, rather than something filled with trauma, questions, and regret.

Deciding to put a dog to sleep is a wrenching choice, but our dogs are completely in our hands. Throughout our lives, they help us through so much. The last, best gift we can give them is to help them through this and give them the most peaceful passage possible.

Better a Week Early Than a Day Late

Now we come to perhaps the most agonizing question of all: How do you know when it's time? Assuming you and your vet have determined that euthanasia is the next step, how do you know if it's time to make the call?

"Oh, you'll know," say your neighbor, your Aunt Sally, and your coworker. They're all seeking to comfort you, so they offer this common salve.

The problem with it is that it's rarely true.

When told there'll be such a definitive "you'll know" kind of sign, people wait for something dramatic, like crying, whimpering, shaking, total refusal of food, and the like. (It's not hard to find a reason to postpone something you are dreading, after all.) Unfortunately, by the time they finally see those impossible-to-miss signs, their dog is suffering a great deal.

A wagging tail has led many an owner to postpone the last day. "Look, she wagged at me! She's still enjoying life." Maybe. Maybe not. This is exactly why getting into a pattern of officially tracking your dog's function, purpose, and joy in the senior years is so important. You'll be much more aware that the wag lasted for only thirty seconds, versus the other twenty-three hours, fifty-nine and a half minutes in the day. The suffering didn't stop during the wag; it's just that your friend loves you so very much.

Keep in mind that there is not one exactly right moment for your dog to pass on. In fact, those with the most experience tend to share this mantra: "Better a week early than a day late." That may sound horrible to the uninitiated. How could you give up even one day with your best friend? The answer is that we've seen what it's like when people miss the window and wait too long. Massive suffering can come on quickly. That can mean you've lost the chance for the peaceful, pain-free appointment you were imagining. There's panic and a rush to whichever vet can fit you in — all while some family members might be too far away to get there in time. Having a dog die in the middle of a stressful catastrophe is traumatic for everyone.

Instead, on an ideal last day, your dog can still walk into his own appointment. He's delighted to find he gets a meal of chicken nuggets and cheeseburgers. He's completely aware that his favorite people are all around him, telling him how much they love him. He's not too stressed to take that in.

Is it incredibly difficult and even confusing to walk a dog who's still that "with it" into a last vet appointment? Absolutely. Will you think, *Oh, wait, maybe...*? Yes, you will.

But then you will remind yourself of all the more-subtle ways your dog has indeed been telling you that it's time. No, he's not screaming it. But you're listening to his whispers, because this is your last chance to put his needs above yours. You've arrived at the bridge between quality of life and quality of death, and your dog is so lucky to have you recognize it.

What's a Good Death?

In the dog world we talk a lot about giving our dogs a good quality of life, one that is enriched, safe, and full of love. What people don't tend to talk about is that there's such a thing as "quality of death" too. The word *euthanasia* comes from the Greek: *eu* ("good") + *thanatos* ("death"). But what exactly is a good death? Here are some things to consider:

- A good death is humane and soft. It is like slipping into a warm bath or taking an afternoon nap. It is calm and welcoming.
- A good death is in the arms of someone trusted who is guiding the way. It is not alone.
- A good death has no worry or confusion.
- A good death has no fear or pain.
- A good death is not on the worst day or the hardest one.
- A good death is when there is still recognition, when the dog is not so far gone in fear, pain, distress, or cognition that they do not know who is with them or how they got there.
- A good death is a day early, on the last best day.

Reading a list like this can help when the decision needs to be made. A good death overlaps with a good life.

Once you've made the decision to say goodbye to your dog, you will be flooded with emotions: relief, guilt, anxiety, sadness, gratitude, all at the same time. Understanding that this is normal is the first step — and then the second step is making the appointment.

At Home or at the Vet?

Thankfully, it is easy to schedule a safe, legal euthanasia with a qualified professional. Depending on where you live, you may also have the option of choosing a location: the vet clinic or your home. Lap of Love is a national company that specializes in at-home pet euthanasia, but sometimes your own vet or another local vet will also be willing to travel to you.

For some, opting to put a dog to sleep at home makes all the difference. It's typically less stressful for the dog, because most have some nervousness around the vet clinic. This choice also eliminates a hard car trip, a struggle to walk into the clinic, and awkward interactions with folks who are there — all of which can be stressful for both the dog and the humans. At home, depending on the weather, you might be able to choose to be outdoors in a favorite spot, which feels right to many of us. In your own household, you can more easily create exactly the right atmosphere with music you love, candles, and so on. It's not difficult to include all family members (including other pets if you'd like to) when you stay at home.

For other families, a clinic is the better choice. For them, planning an at-home goodbye may feel like something extra to manage, rather than a trip to the vet where someone else is in charge. For some households, figuring out how to integrate children and other pets into this moment is simply too hard, so it's easier to leave them home and head to the clinic. Sometimes people decide they don't want to have a place in their home that constantly reminds them of that sad event. Others might feel that the spot would become such a spiritual touchstone that if they had to move, they'd experience the loss all over again.

As for cost, that can vary based on where you live and which options you choose. The national average is between $100 and $300, but an at-home euthanasia with ashes returned to you might be $700 or more.

Take a moment to think through which option will work best for your family.

Making the Phone Call

Despite it being difficult to make the decision, a planned death is far less traumatic and stressful for both your dog and you. Here are some things to keep in mind as you schedule the appointment:

- If you have a good relationship with your vet, then you will have come to this decision with their help and experience on board. That means this call will be expected and they will help you through it.
- If somehow you are forced to use a vet who's not well aware of your history with your dog (and the fact that you've considered this decision thoroughly), you may be offered another exam for the purpose of discussing different treatments or medications. It's okay to decline more intervention. It doesn't mean you don't love your dog! You are advocating for quality of life and a good death.
- Sometimes Lap of Love books up a week in advance, so if you're set on an at-home appointment make

sure to call to check availability, even if you haven't 100 percent decided on a day. Once you make this decision, it's typical to want to move ahead within a day or two.

Being Your Dog's Rock

Once you've made the call, there is one very important way that you can make the walk along the road to the rainbow bridge way better for your dog, and it's by being a soothing presence — their rock — throughout. We humans are so lucky to have this option of creating a calm passage for our dogs. The last thing we want to do is ruin that by letting our own deep anguish upset our dog.

Of course you're going to feel beyond sad. But just remember how tuned in to you your dog has always been. If, as she declines, you are sadder than she's ever seen, she's going to get scared and wonder what the heck is going on. Her anxiety will skyrocket. If instead you are calm, reassuring, and loving, those emotions will guide her. She'll settle in next to you and feel all is well.

You'll have plenty of time to mourn afterward. But when you're in her presence, try to reach down deep and create beautiful moments for the two of you.

What to Expect at the Vet

Here's something to take to heart if you're approaching this big moment for the first time: Some of the most strongly delivered notes of appreciation to veterinarians come from people who've just had to put their dog to sleep. Why?

Because, far from acting like this is just another day at work, these professionals tenderly lead us through this challenging moment, sitting with us through the tears. Many people are surprised by how much support and care they feel from these folks at that moment. So don't be afraid to lean on them! They have done this before, and they will do everything they can to help you and your dog through this passage.

The first thing you can ask from them is to walk you through their process ahead of time — either on the phone or in person — so that you know exactly what to anticipate. *That's incredibly important because every clinic is different, and there are even regional variances in approach.* To give you a general idea, here is a possible scenario:

- **Quietest time of day.** If they can, most vets like to schedule this appointment for a time when the clinic is not as busy, because everything is simpler when there are fewer distractions and interactions.

- **Dedicated room.** Most vets have a special room they use for these appointments that is quiet and darkened. They might provide blankets or bedding and comfortable seating.

- **Ample time.** If they can, most vets want to give you as much time as you need for this process. The actual euthanasia only takes a few minutes, but they want to give you time to sit with your dog before and after if you'd like.

- **Sedation first?** Find out if your vet's process is to sedate your dog before the actual euthanasia, which we recommend. It may add a bit to the bill, but this typically ensures that the entire process will be very smooth.

- **Separation for IV catheter placement?** The vet will almost always choose to place an IV catheter in the dog. The catheter is a secure connection to the bloodstream, meaning that the drugs can take effect quickly and smoothly. Sometimes vets prefer to bring the dog into the back to place the catheter because this is the hard part: The needle poke can sometimes be challenging (if the dog is very old, dehydrated, or very anxious). If you strongly wish to stay by your dog's side the whole time, that's something to ask about.

- **Private time.** The vet will likely offer to leave the room to give you private time to say your goodbyes before a sedative is given. (After it takes full effect, your dog will not regain consciousness.)

- **Getting sleepy.** Once a dog receives the sedative, they usually get sleepy very quickly. Your dog will likely lie down in a cozy spot right next to you, and you can snuggle and talk to him.

- **The injection.** Once the dog is in a peaceful sleep, it's time. The vet will let you know they're going to start the process and will typically administer a large amount of barbiturate (a depressant that suppresses the cardiovascular and respiratory systems) through an IV catheter.

- **Slowing breathing and heartbeat.** Within a minute or two, you will feel your dog's breathing peacefully slowing as he drifts off. After listening to the heart to ensure it has stopped, the vet will let you know when your dog has passed on.

(Again, each vet handles this appointment slightly differently, and we highly suggest you use this list as a guide as you ask your own clinic staff what their exact process is.)

Vets know that this is not the moment to expect you to deal with paperwork, payment, or decisions about remains. Typically they will go over all that beforehand or a few days later.

While some people have a special spot where they'd like to bury their dog's body, most owners choose to have their dog cremated. For an extra charge, you can have an individual cremation, and you'll receive your dog's ashes back in a few weeks. You might opt for a pretty box with your dog's name, an urn, or just the ashes for you to scatter somewhere special.

What we hope to convey here is that while it is sad to say goodbye, the actual process is not something to fear. In the vast majority of cases, a planned, scheduled euthanasia is smooth and peaceful. It is very much like simply watching your dog fall into a deep and beautiful sleep as they're held in the arms of their favorite people.

What About the Puppy During Your Senior's Last Day?

If you have already added a puppy to the family, you'll want to think through how to manage her on your senior's last day. Owners are filled with questions about whether the puppy should be present, whether she'll know what's going on, and whether she'll grieve. There's one answer to all of this: This is a moment to focus on yourself and your senior. Your puppy will be okay.

Ideally, your loved ones can step in to help, possibly taking your puppy off your hands for a bit. Maybe your friends can take the pup during the vet appointment, and your neighbors can pitch in over the first few days to tire out the pup. While some folks will immediately want to have the comfort and distraction of their puppy after their dog passes, others may need a day or two to sink into grief away from puppy energy. Don't be afraid to ask for what you need! New experiences with trusted folks are wonderful for puppies.

Grieving

The day of the appointment will come, and it will be excruciatingly painful to your heart. In your mind you will know it is the best decision, and you will have prepared as best you can. But don't be surprised when you still feel utterly shattered.

Be gentle with yourself. There's simply nothing like this loss. It's often confusing to people that they can feel more gutted by the death of their dog than they have been by the death of a human they loved. That's very common! What's "easier" about losing a parent who lived a few states away is that you don't have constant reminders that life as you knew it has forever changed. But as you move through your days after your dog dies — waking up in no rush, answering the door when nobody barked, sitting on the couch without a head in your lap, going to sleep in an empty room — every moment feels different. (It's also true that we tend to experience a powerfully unconditional love with our dogs, while our human relationships are more complex.)

There are some things that can help. For sure, take some time off from your regular obligations. Lean on the support of others, seek out grief counseling offered through your local shelter, and speak openly about how you feel.

One tip from those who've been through this a lot is to try to take a small amount of time each day to allow yourself to feel the sadness. These structured grief sessions can be healing and enable you to function better between them. Journaling, crying, listening to a song that reminds you of your pet — all these things are great for grief sessions.

There are also many ways to memorialize your dog, to capture that unique spirit so that on some level you will always have a way to feel close to your old friend:

- Create a slideshow you can watch on your phone whenever you need to.
- Write out your favorite memories.
- Make a book, either by hand or online.
- Collect everybody's best stories about your dog and read them aloud every now and then.
- Have a backyard memorial service where you tell stories, offer prayers, sing that goofy song you made up for him, look at a photo board, and eat your dog's favorite snacks!
- Enlarge your very favorite photo of your dog and put it in a special spot in your home, with a candle

nearby. Go there when you want to sit with your dog.

- Find a shelter or rescue group and donate or volunteer every year on your dog's birthday.
- Go to Etsy.com and see all the ways you can creatively memorialize your dog: custom stones for your garden, necklaces, mugs, wind chimes, bracelets, and on and on.

While all these things can help ease your grief, the best healer of all is time. One day, for sure, the transformation will happen: You'll be reminded of your dog, and instead of it feeling like a gut punch, you'll smile.

Chapter Six

Starting the Next Chapter

Eventually, time will help mend your heart after the loss of the incredible dog who's been by your side for years. Want to know a secret, though? A puppy can help time work its magic a lot faster.

If you opted to delay adding a puppy to the household until your senior passed, that option is now back on the table. Is this the right time to start again?

Some folks instinctively shy away from the thought at first, thinking they could never "replace" their old friend. But, happily, replacement is not the goal. Your senior dog was one of a kind, and your relationship was too. A new puppy is a chance to embark on a different journey. You now have time, energy, and love that has nowhere to go. You can choose to build something new.

Sometimes people feel that, while they know they want to get a puppy at some point, it would somehow be disloyal to their old dog to rush into it right away. After all, if they have a puppy in the house, they'll be playing and laughing and cuddling and…feeling happy. Shouldn't they spend more time resting in the sadness and mourning their friend?

Nobody can answer the question "How much time do I need to grieve?" for anyone else. But if you're thinking your old dog would be sad if your devastation were replaced with joy, it might help to close your eyes and really consider what that sweet old friend would want for you. You both know what you had together. Committing to feel lonely and depressed for a longer time doesn't add legitimacy or depth to that story.

Conflicted Feelings Are Normal

A brand-new puppy can be a powerful balm, cheering everyone when that seemed an impossible task. A puppy is a phenomenal distraction that's guaranteed to get you up and about, outside and around other people. For many who've just lost their dog, that's an immediate lifesaver, filling an all-too-quiet house with activity and laughter.

However, every now and then, folks find some unexpected feelings surfacing after the initial puppy honeymoon. They might find themselves thinking:

- *Ugh! This is hard! My older dog never acted like this as a puppy!*
- *Help! I don't love the puppy as much as I loved my older dog!*

These emotions can bring on a fresh wave of grief. You miss your perfect old friend. You may realize, belatedly, that somewhere in there you kind of expected the puppy to fill that giant hole — the hole that was dug and molded over a dozen years of life together — immediately. But these feelings of disappointment are in fact a natural part of your grieving process. The best thing to do is to fully recognize that this phase is normal, and let yourself — and your puppy — off the hook.

First of all, *of course* this puppy behavior seems over the top and feels like way too much work! You've been living with a senior for years! Puppyhood is so intense, most of us later block out the hard parts (kind of like childbirth), and even a year afterward, we don't remember just how frustrated we were. By the time our dogs are seniors, calmly napping at our feet, never jumping up, and never chewing furniture, we truly don't believe they ever did that stuff. Honestly, though: They did. The sooner you let yourself remember that at five months of age, your old dog wasn't a saint yet, the sooner you'll be able to really open yourself to and enjoy this new puppy.

Now on to the worry that you don't love the new puppy as much as you loved your senior....Ha! Well, again, that's normal! Relationships take time and shared experiences to develop. Your senior dog had years and years of those with you, and your relationship deepened with each adventure. You are just getting to know this little soul.

So don't worry. All of this is part of grieving. The healthiest thing you can do is allow yourself to feel those pesky negative emotions and talk about them openly. And as for your puppy, here are some things to try if you want to jump-start that emotional connection:

- **Savor one-on-one time.** Rather than sitting around at home missing your senior and feeling that contrast, go somewhere new with your puppy. Take a puppy class. Find a puppy friend up the street and watch the cutest playdate you've ever seen. These moments offer fresh ways to create your bond.

- **Train something new.** Puppies can physically do things that our sweet old seniors couldn't do anymore, so leaning into those activities can feel like a wonderful new beginning. Fun training is a great example. Start by teaching "touch" and "spin," and note how easily that ache-free young body can respond with joy. Introduce rolling over and jumping in and out of a box. Having fun? Now you're on your way.

- **Keep a journal.** Puppy journaling can be cathartic and will be wonderful to look back on later. Note every milestone, playdate, new trick, vet visit, and shredded couch pillow. Take pictures and record it all. As you're doing that, you'll find you're training your brain and your heart to really "see" this new baby.

Over the first few months as you get to know the new puppy, you may keep getting thrown off by behaviors and personality traits that contrast with your old senior: *Hmm. This is different from Sparky.* At first, it may take you aback, but eventually you'll see those very differences as an incredible gift. They're the signal that you have a brand-new journey ahead of you. Every dog has something to teach us. What will this unique spirit bring out in you?

Starting the Next Chapter

A Final Thought: The Magical Tapestry

If you get them talking, almost every dog person will eventually tell you about their "heart dog."

It's shorthand for the dog who made us feel so deeply connected we were never alone. It's the dog who was by our side through it all, who knew us inside and out, who made everything better just by resting their chin on our foot. The two of us were completely in sync: kindred souls who found each other against impossible odds.

It is incredibly hard, after losing that dog, to imagine you could ever have something like that again. Even the thought of looking for a new dog can feel like a betrayal.

We urge you to try.

The truth is that the best predictor of having a "heart dog" is that you've had one before. We, along with so many other dog professionals, wound up in this work because of that one heart dog who moved us so much we wanted to spend our lives thinking about that extraordinary canine-human connection.

Imagine our surprise when another "heart dog" landed in our lap a few years later. And then another.

When that happens, does it take away from the magic of that original best friend? Does it make that relationship less special? If you open yourself up to a new puppy and then find an extraordinary bond there, does it somehow lessen what you had with your senior?

It does not. In fact, it turns it into something even bigger.

Here's how we think of it: It's all part of the magical tapestry we weave through a lifetime of loving and living with these incredible creatures. While our relationship with a new puppy isn't the same as the one with our old friend, it rhymes, and echoes. Every now and then it does that so much that we'd swear our old heart dog is in the room, whispering in our new dog's ear. It's like our old friend is actively part of this connection, cheerleading our aching soul to enjoy these fleeting moments, and to love again.

If that sounds crazy to you, maybe you haven't had enough dogs yet! To those of us who've opened up again and again to new dogs after loss, the idea that we are in fact walking around with a pack of invisible friends feels just about right. Maybe you're thinking that's just a story we tell ourselves to feel better as we mourn loss. Okay, we'll wait. We'll wait until the first time you realize your old friend is whispering to your puppy about just how to snuggle up with you.

Over time, the rhymes, echoes, and whispers of our dear departed senior start to bring only smiles as we realize the cracks in our broken heart seem to have created openings for more love, more joy.

So this is our best advice: Lean into this new puppy. Let her make you laugh again. Let her remind you not to take anything for granted. She will now carry the torch, and the next chapter together begins.

Acknowledgments

From Kathy and Helen

This book owes its existence to all the dogs who joined our families as if on a mission to prove that there's always more love ahead — especially after the loss of a particularly wonderful dog — if you stay open to it. We hope this book helps readers along that same path of joyful discovery.

Of course, there are exceptional humans who contributed to this book too. First up is Kim Brophey, because the seed for this book was planted at her Family Dog Mediation conference, where the two of us listened to one another's mirror-image presentations with glee, hugged the second we met, and essentially outlined this book over the coffee break. Next on the gratitude list: our trusted agent, Joan Brookbank, who embraced this topic from the get-go, and the wonderful team at New World Library who took it on, with particular thanks to Kristen Cashman for her thoughtful edit of the manuscript. We had helpful early readers (including the Third Act women and Dr. Veronica Jarvinen).

We can't forget Terry Klima, whose insights were the reason this book moved immediately to the top of the to-write project list. Finally, we're both absurdly lucky to have husbands and daughters who cheer us on. Without their faith in us, and their support for the work, this book would still just be a fuzzy idea.

A special dedication from Helen

I am particularly grateful to the senior and hospice dogs who've landed at my doorstep — 250 of them at this writing — and taught me so much. Even when my time with them has been brief, it's been a gift to know them and to love them. They have enriched my understanding of what it means to live a good life and how important it is to have a good death. Inevitably, when the end comes, I hold those dogs close and help them to pass on, free from suffering. I wrote this book, in part, to honor them.

Even more, though, this book is for my mom, who taught me never to take no for an answer and to question everything. Last year, I was at her side as she died slowly, painfully, from cancer. I advocated for her as best I could within the system, but the death she experienced was not the kind she wanted or deserved. She would have chosen to go on her last best day, without agony, surrounded by all of us who love her. Unfortunately, she did not have that option. I so wish that my mom could have had the same peaceful, loving, and calm passing that I am able to give the animals in my care when it's their time.

When people tell me they don't feel right talking about euthanasia for their beloved dog, I think about my mom. I know she'd be so proud of this book and love its message and guidance. She'd wish that readers would try to become comfortable with discussions about death, that they'd help their dogs live their very best lives right until the end, and that they would embrace the incredible gift we have in the ability to choose for them a dignified death, free of suffering.

Index

acupuncture, 23
adult dogs: as good senior matches, 84–85; introductions, 86–88; play behavior of, 84; puppy additions vs., 81–84; puppy playdates with, 67; selecting for adoption, 85–86; as senior friends, 61
agency, 56, 60
aging, symptoms of, 7–8
air mattresses, 14–15
alertness, assessing, 26, 29
American Veterinary Society of Animal Behavior Position Statement on Puppy Socialization (2018), 53
anesthesia, 24
anticipatory grief, 92–93
anxiety: during euthanasia, 105; increased, 8, 9, 11–12, 17; reducing, in senior dogs, 17–18
appetite, changes in, 8
arthritis, 10, 94
at-home exams, weekly, 6–7

bad breath, 8
bed, access to, 12, 13
belly bands, 16–17
biopsies, 24
biting, 88
bloodwork, 7
body language: paying attention to, 5–6; during senior and new adult dog interaction, 87; during senior and puppy interaction, 60–61, 63
bones, 40, 73, 88
boundaries, 64
boxes, jumping into/out of, 116
Brophey, Kim, 66
brushing, 6
bucket lists, 93

chew toys, 40–41, 47
chewing, 12, 35, 36, 39–41, 68
cleaning station, 16
coat, dulling of, 8
coexistence areas, 11
cognitive decline, 8, 15, 26, 28, 62
"come," 53–54

Index

commands. *See* cues
companion-animal end-of-life doulas, 21
confusion, 8
connection, puppy training for, 53–56
constipation, 7
"correcting," 40, 64. *See also* cues; puppies — training of
crates, 46–47, 48, 72
cremation, 108
cuddle time, 14, 92
cues: "come," 53–54; "down," 53; "find it!" 44–45, 55, 74; "off," 55; "oops," 40; "sit," 54, 61, 64, 74; "spin," 53, 55, 116; "touch," 54–55, 61, 64, 74, 116; "yes!" 53, 54

death: good, 102; "natural," 98–99; Western aversion to acknowledging, 3, 91–92. *See also* euthanasia
dental cleanings, 24
diapers, doggy, 16–17, 71
diary-keeping, 24–25. *See also* journaling
diet, 41
digging, 35, 68
dog care schedule, daily, 78
dog trainers, 87
dogs: "heart dogs," 117–18; pain and survival mechanisms of, 98; resource-guarding behavior of, 88. *See also* adult dogs; puppies; senior dogs
doulas, end-of-life, 21
"down," 53

ear infections, early detection of, 6
eating habits: assessing, 25, 29; changes in, 8
eating/drinking areas, 11
elimination habits: assessing, 26, 29; changes in, 7; in puppies, 36. *See also* potty areas, access to; potty training
emergencies, 19, 95
encouragement, 17–18
end-of-life discussions, 20–21, 31, 97–98
end-of-life doulas, 21
enrichment activities, 68
Etsy.com, 111
euthanasia: appointment for, 104–5; cost of, 104; deciding upon, 102; etymology of, 102; as a good death, 102; grieving after, 109–11; human emotional support during, 105; location of, 103–4; medical intervention vs., 95–96, 104; "natural" death vs., 98–99; planned, advantages of, 99–102, 108; process of, at vet's office, 105–8; sedation during, 106–7
exams, weekly at-home, 6–7
exercise, for senior dogs, 4
eye contact, 39, 42, 53, 74
eyes, cloudy, 8
eyesight, assessing, 26, 29

family: college kids, 96; daily dog care schedule involving, 78–79; planned euthanasia and, 99, 101, 103; senior dogs as part of, 1–2; senior end-of-life discussions involving, 95, 96; senior supervision by, 14. *See also* home environment
Family Dog Mediation course, 66
fearfulness, 49, 77
fetch game, 64

123

financial considerations, 21, 96, 104
"find it!" 44–45, 55, 74
floor futons, 15
food: areas for, 11; guarding of, 88; puppy training using, 42–44; senior access to, 12, 13; during senior and puppy interaction, 71–73. *See also* food toys; treats
food toys: for puppy socialization, 68; puppy training using, 43, 47; during senior sunset, 92; during senior and puppy interaction, 73
foster homes, adopting from, 85–86
fostering-to-adopt, 86
function, assessing, 25–26, 29, 97–98, 100–101

gates. *See* pen/gate setup
grief: anticipatory, dealing with, 92–93; pain of, 109–10; preparing for, 79; puppies acquired during time of, 113–18; suggestions for dealing with, 110–11
grief counseling, 110
growling, 64, 88

hair-drying, 49–50
hearing: assessing, 26, 29; senior losses in, 7, 62
"heart dogs," 117–18
home environment: adult dog matches for, 84–85; euthanasia at, vs. vet's office, 103–4; for puppies, 35–37; for senior and new adult dog cohabitation, 88; for senior and puppy cohabitation, 59–61, 63–65, 68–70. *See also* family; senior dogs — home environment adjustments for
hospice-certified technicians, 21
human play, 67–68

immunizations, 52–53
inclusion, 13–14
incontinence: as aging symptom, 7, 15, 70; management of, 15–17, 70–71
interventions, 24
isolation, 13

joint issues, 10
journaling, 24–25, 79, 110, 116
joy, assessing, 28, 30, 97–98, 100–101
jumping, 35

Karl Hack, the, 66
kidney failure, 94
Kongs, 6. *See also* food toys

Lap of Love, 103, 104–5
laser therapy, 23
leash training, 44–46, 74
limits, new, 18
Lowe's, 77
lumps: appearance of, 8; early detection of, 6; removing, 24

matting, 6
medical intervention, 94–98, 104
medications, for pain, 22–23
memorials, 94, 110–11
Miller, Pat, 40
mobility: assessing, 25, 29; senior difficulties with, 7, 10, 11–12
mouthing, 35
muscle atrophy, 8, 10

Index

nails, long, 6
name recognition, 53
nanny dogs, 67
naps, 47
Nature's Miracle, 70
navigation difficulties, 7
"no," 40, 64
nonslip flooring, 10–11, 26
nutrition: for puppies, 41; for senior dogs, 4–5. *See also* food

observation, 75–76
"off," 55
one-level living, 11–12
"oops," 40
other dogs: puppy leash training using, 46; puppy socialization with, 50–52; unvaccinated, 52–53

pain: euthanasia and minimization of, 99; rapid onset of, 101
pain, assessing, 30
pain management, 20, 22–23, 96–98
pee pads, 16, 70–71
pen/gate setup, 59–60, 63, 69–70, 72, 88
pet insurance, 7, 21, 96
physical therapy, 23
play: human play, 67–68; puppy play, 40–41, 51–52; senior dogs and, 5, 11, 61–62, 84. *See also* food toys; toys
playdates, 65–66, 67, 116
potty areas, access to, 12, 13
potty training, 37–39, 70
pup cups, 92
puppies: adding after senior's death, 113–18; adult dog addition vs., 81–84; advice about, 33–34; connecting with, 115–16; crates for, 46–47, 48; feeding, 41, 47; home environment for, 35–37; play behavior of, 84; quick-start guide to, 34; senior dogs and, 33, 61–65, 93–94, 108–9; sleeping with, 47–48; socializing, 48–53, 76–78, 83; tiring out, for best senior-puppy interaction, 65–68; transition to human environment, 34–35; trust-building with, 35, 46. *See also* puppies — training of; senior and puppy experience
puppies — training of: for chewing behavior, 39–41; for connection, 53–56, 73–74, 115–16; for crate use, 46–47; leash training, 44–46, 74; potty training, 37–39, 70; treats for, 39, 42–44, 46–47, 74. *See also* cues
"puppy apartment," 35–37, 42–43, 68, 69
puppy classes, 52, 116
puppy friends, 51–52, 65–66
purpose, assessing, 26–28, 29–30, 97–98, 100–101

quality-of-life considerations: assessing, 24–28; diary-keeping for, 24–25; discussions about, 20–21; function, 25–26, 29, 31; joy, 28, 30, 31; medical care and, 22–23; purpose, 26–28, 29–30, 31; questionnaire for, 28–30

ramps, 14
resource guarding, 88

125

rest areas, 11
rolling over, 116
rugs, nonslip, 10, 26

sedation: during euthanasia, 106–7; senior dogs and, 24
senior dogs: adult dog friends of, 61; adult dog matches for, 84–85; adult dogs introduced to, 86–88; aging symptoms, 7–8, 62; decline of, 78–79; defined, 2–3; easing anxiety in, 17–18; health maintenance for, 3–7; human reaction to aging of, 1–2, 3; inclusive area for, 13–14; medical procedures and, 24; memorializing, 110–11; pain management for, 20, 22–24; puppies acquired during lifetime of, 33, 61–65 (*see also* senior and puppy experience); puppies acquired following death of, 113–18. See also quality-of-life considerations; senior dogs — home environment adjustments for; senior and puppy experience
senior dogs — end-of-life process: anticipatory grief and, 92–93; learning to savor, 91, 93–94; medical intervention and, 94–98; pain management and, 96–98; pain of, 91–92; puppies and, 93–94, 108–9; support network during, 109. See also euthanasia
senior dogs — home environment adjustments for: cuddle time, 14; importance of, 8–9; incontinence management, 15–17, 70–71; nonslip flooring, 10–11, 26; one-level living, 11–12; "senior space," 12–14, 68–69; sleeping arrangements, 14–15
"senior space," 12–14, 68–69
senior and puppy experience: alternative puppy entertainment during, 65–68; boundary-setting in, 64; challenges of, 58; feeding arrangements, 71–73; home environment adjustments for, 59–61, 63–65, 68–71; ideal picture of, 57, 79–80; introductions, 59–61; poop/pee management, 70–71; puppy energy and, 61–65; puppy socialization during, 76–78; senior decline and, 78–79, 80, 93–94; senior euthanasia and, 108–9; support network during, 75, 78–79, 109; timing and, 58; walk arrangements, 73–76
seniorhood, defined, 3
shelters, adopting from, 86
"sit," 54, 61, 64, 74
skin infections, early detection of, 6
skittishness, 49, 77
sleeping habits: assessing, 26, 29; changes in, 8
snapping, 64, 88
"sniffaris," 4, 61, 75, 88
sniffing, 51, 68
"spin," 53, 55, 116
staircases, 11–12
stamina, decreased, 8
stress reduction, for senior dogs, 5–6
stuffed dog toy, realistic, 66
suffering. *See* pain
support network, 75, 78–79, 109

Index

Toppls, 6, 43, 47, 68. *See also* food toys
"touch," 54–55, 61, 64, 74, 116
toys, 40–41, 43, 66, 88. *See also* food toys
transition areas, 11
treat pouches, 42
treats: during puppy socialization, 50; puppy training using, 39, 42–44, 46–47, 68, 74; for senior dogs, 5; during senior and puppy interaction, 61, 64, 68, 73; during senior sunset, 92
tug game, 64

ultrasounds, 7
urinary tract infections (UTIs), 7, 15, 17

vacuuming, 49–50
vet clinics, emergency, 19, 95
veterinarians: client preparedness for visits to, 20–24; cost of, 21; end-of-life discussions with, 97–98; euthanasia at office of, 103–4, 105–8; relationship with, 18–19, 104; wellness visits with, 7, 18
veterinary industry, 21
vision loss: assessing, 26, 29; senior difficulties with, 7, 62

walks: leash walks, 44–46; during potty training, 39; for puppy socialization, 51, 67, 68; during senior sunset, 16, 92; during senior and puppy interaction, 64, 73–76; "sniffaris," 4, 61, 75, 88
watch parties, 75–76
water, access to, 12, 13
Welcoming Your Puppy from Planet Dog (Callahan), 34, 53

X-rays, 7

"yes!" 53, 54

127

About the Authors

Certified as a dog trainer (CPDT-KA) and a family dog mediator (LFDM), **Kathy Callahan** specializes in puppies. She has fostered almost 250 of them in the past decade, and her dog training business, PupStart, is focused on puppyhood.

Kathy is the author of *Welcoming Your Puppy from Planet Dog: How to Go Beyond Training and Raise Your Best Friend* and *101 Rescue Puppies: One Family's Story of Fostering Dogs, Love, and Trust*. Kathy also writes on training and behavior for *Whole Dog Journal*. Her podcast, *Pick of the Litter*, covers the ideas and approaches that truly help people and their dogs live more happily together.

About the Authors

Kathy lives in Alexandria, Virginia, with her husband, Tom. Their current dogs, Mojo, George, Kreacher, and Clover, all started out as fosters, but soon revealed themselves to be Callahans — perhaps aided by the whispers of those beloved family members who came before them: Ben, Shadow, Kela, Piper, Zoe, Eli, Rocket, and Nala.

Check out Kathy's website at PuppyPicks.com and her puppy fostering and training adventures on Facebook (Kathy Gord Callahan) and Instagram @puppy.picks.

Helen St. Pierre is the founder of the senior rescue organization Old Dogs Go To Helen and the owner and operator of No Monkey Business Dog Training. Helen is certified as a professional dog trainer (CPDT-KSA), a dog behavior consultant (CDBC), and a family dog mediator (LFDM). She has been training dogs for over twenty years and handles everything from basic obedience and service dog training to serious cases of aggression. She is a licensed Dogs & Storks educator, a licensed Dogs & Toddlers educator, and a certified AKC evaluator. Helen is also certified as a Peaceful Euthanasia Professional and an End-of-Life Companion Animal Doula.

Helen and her husband, Jake, live with their daughters and pets on a wonderful twenty-acre property outside Concord, New Hampshire, which also serves as the sanctuary for Old Dogs Go To Helen. All told, there are dogs, cats, horses, pigs, donkeys, goats, and parrots happily living out their days in that beautiful setting.

To learn more about supporting her mission, check out Helen's rescue website at OldDogsGoToHelen.com.

NEW WORLD LIBRARY is dedicated to publishing books and other media that inspire and challenge us to improve the quality of our lives and the world.

We are a socially and environmentally aware company. We recognize that we have an ethical responsibility to our readers, our authors, our staff members, and our planet.

We serve our readers by creating the finest publications possible on personal growth, creativity, spirituality, wellness, and other areas of emerging importance. We serve our authors by working with them to produce and promote quality books that reach a wide audience. We serve New World Library employees with generous benefits, significant profit sharing, and constant encouragement to pursue their most expansive dreams.

We print our books with soy-based ink on paper from sustainably managed forests. We power our Northern California office with solar energy, and we respectfully acknowledge that it is located on the ancestral lands of the Coast Miwok Indians. We also contribute to nonprofit organizations working to make the world a better place for us all.

Our products are available wherever books are sold.

customerservice@NewWorldLibrary.com
Phone: 415-884-2100 or 800-972-6657
Orders: Ext. 110
Fax: 415-884-2199
NewWorldLibrary.com

Scan below to access our newsletter
and learn more about our books and authors.